SELECTED PO

SELECTED POEMS 1977–1992

Judith Kazantzis

SINCLAIR-STEVENSON

First published in Great Britain in 1995
by Sinclair-Stevenson
an imprint of Reed Consumer Books Ltd
Michelin House, 81 Fulham Road, London SW3 6RB
and Auckland, Melbourne, Singapore and Toronto

British Library Cataloguing in Publication Data
A CIP catalogue record for this book is available from the British Library.

ISBN 1 85619 552 X

Typeset by Deltatype, Ellesmere Port, South Wirral
Printed and bound in Great Britain by Cox & Wyman Ltd, Reading, Berkshire

For Arthur and Miranda

Acknowledgements

The poems in this selection were originally published by the following:

Minefield – Sidgwick & Jackson, 1977
The Wicked Queen – Sidgwick & Jackson, 1980
Touch Papers – Allison & Busby, 1982
Let's Pretend – Virago, 1984
Flame Tree – Methuen, 1988
A Poem for Guatemala – originally published by Bedlam Press, then by The Greville Press, 1988
The Rabbit Magician Plate – Sinclair-Stevenson, 1992

Uncollected poems appeared in *Poetry Review*, *Ambit*, *Verse* and *South East Arts Anthology*.

Contents

ix

from
Minefield (1977)

home

trapped in the laid-out garden
the fixed sky, the blank green
static hedge, the heavy marching chestnuts
under the leaf inlay, the burial of summer
the breathless pyre

I could have taken a bus to the sea
easily: walked through the front gate
there were plenty of cinemas
I lay on the clipped grass
and watched elderly clouds

there was no permission needed. I
could have jumped ship, seen
all the continents

I walked gravel paths, round and
round in the garden. I trod
moss. I saw love in the mist
roses, fuchsia, larkspur and each year
the eminent tiger-lily

travellers light

my love, do you hear
the seasonal voice of travellers light
in my sleepy afternoon dark
who come up behind us —
my arm at your arm, your thigh between my thighs
three pillows for our two heads
pushed up to all soft angles
I am at the back of the beyond
a thread of conversation like a ship's wake

2

I lean out in my marigold silk —
below, you are planting the red bulbs
of tulips. I feel the earth through your fingers
your damp hair, the weight of night
crouched on your back
and the final sidling noises of birds
in the roof over the lighted bedroom

cuckoo mouth

the queen of the mutton brass arms
says to me constantly
a whisper behind closed doors
don't move
I have let the dogs out – don't move

I watched her in the kitchen
scrubbing potatoes
she sets out cakes as neat as apples
angelica good as gold
she makes dinner for a hundred
I mentioned the whiteness of her hands
she looked at the clock
the queen is my real mother

and another time – in the garden
I was hunting for groundsel
the queen reached to me from the trees
embracing my shoulders in her long bending arms
I had forgotten her that morning –
and like a fairground horse
the sun began to gallop in the sky

her face was as long as a leaf
she was telling the sun to canter
I ran for the house
dropping the plants across the lawn
but the queen is my real mother

from the attic I watched her
sweep up with long strokes

today the mother has gone to market
packing turnips into the boot of the car
and the house is mine

shadows of trees lie on the field
whistle of a starling
the house . . . and the kitchen?
excuse me, I whisper to the clock
to the cakes, I must eat before she comes back
and I do

my mouth is greedy as a cuckoo's mouth
twittering for dinner, dinner, dinner
bigger than can be fed reasonably
I don't stop at the cakes, at the clock
or the hundred dinners, the kitchen, the attic
the house, the garden, but
I stop at the gate
there are two dogs
as stone as lions

don't move
I am your real mother now
don't move
as good as gold
I have inside me all that you treasure
I have stolen the queen's goods
let us bargain

stationary eyes
they prick their ears for that majesty
the gate grows weeds
and I die, die of hunger
telling the time by dandelions
and craving the brown field

oh when will she return
the woman with the brown arms
who cooks with a will and does the washing-up
and makes the beds
and sees to the garden
and catches apples from the squat orchard
and says that one day I will have breasts

I have forgotten her name
but she was mistress of the animals
long time she's gone to market
she's forgotten, she's forgotten

breechchild

this child was a breech
riding like a hell-hound between my thighs
he cracked a particular little whip in the marrow
   of my bones
causing a flurry of agitated sighs

what will he come to?
he's gone now, riding hell for leather
across the hard sand of the estuary
flogging the damn little beach pony
as if it was Bucephalus

I have milk clotted in two enormous breasts
because he bit the nipples raw
spat out the blood
and weaned himself in disgust

film

underground
under the kitchen, where they skin rabbits
throwing the skins away to the old cat –
I will have your ridge of scarlet again
and again, expecting no words.
my ear rings where you sucked the sea salt
like a monster.
two spaniels bark in the morning

how she lay, asking to be peeled
her breasts half filling their steep white cups
then – it was an old film – they cut to
the pretty afterwards
but in the night, my night
on the catacomb floor, shiny film
falls and curls from the projector

acquaintance

ice round here is thin
daisy ice, like the buttercups under your chin
that pretends you like butter

under the sky
the elms are really huge sprouts, or greens
unpulled on a frosty day
and now out of reach

in this allotment
watching birds
behind the tractor shed
I found an old pond
jammed with petrol cans
and brown broken rushes
a duck flew up with a squawk
in the corner of my eye
watching me
I saw the bull
his great horned forehead
his frozen white-lashed eyes

walking from lap to knee
of the downs, I jokingly
looked for him
— and saw his troll face among the heifers
I cleared out
his lady cantered by the barb wire
the old gent plodded behind on porridge plate feet
a mountain of lard
with two hairs of metal
to keep his great tonnage as
passive as a butter dish

one a.m., november

the vibrant, experienced dishwasher
drums in the night
the cat bunches on the very edge of the ping-pong table
lulled
by the swish and wallow of saucepans

putting my feet sleepily
in the caftan of a chic and rumpled night
down to a Moorish pink-breasted
kitchen, the light wrapped in
kingfisher colour horn

the explosions and whistles
right in my ear upped and drove me
to see to my temple
this electric sanctuary of greasy water
its bright red oneeye says nix
but the interior seems

panicky: a possible murderous grind
of combative metal: clicks
of self destruct
I don't know the speech

and they were fireworks, and this temple
drums on
may it tear its veil not, before morning
the cat stares
there is no god

the song of Punch on the beach

on the windy whistly saturday beach
oyez oyez I say I say
ladies gents and kiddies I give you
that remarkable, that incorrigible
the uniquely brutal
wife batterer to millions
Punch!
dog Toby laughs to see such fun
and the sea goes, scrunch

on the wipey ripply sunday beach
he's at it again
with his nutcracker chin and his shiny nose
he's doing his baby's nut, and the wife
and the cops and the neighbours
are biting the sand
dog Toby laughs to see such fun
and the sea goes, scrunch

on monday's beach all sweetpapery
empty as a pepsi can
the rain beats like a truncheon
he beat her up at the turn of the tide
and the little kids laughed to see such fun
and the bodies of all concerned are gone
the *News of the World* is out to sea
and the sea goes, scrunch

sunday in the country

in the hour of sponge cake
adulterous husbands circle like bovver boys
full of aggro, eyeing prey.
under the mouths and breasts of roses
we drink tea. the kettle hisses dreams

travelling hand
under the pink bower
lips my waist, mouth at my breast
I am out at sea, legs
float free in the water, hand held.
I screw up your curls, bite
the heat of your neck

for a moment I am as fast and liquid
as my lost cat
till sins grumble back

from
The Wicked Queen (1980)

The wicked queen

You doubt me?
Lovely therefore I am,
loveliest of them all makes me Goddess
(the king who also wants God uses his mirror
for shaving in; and no-one thinks
him odd; he swears when he cuts himself).

Black hair
is serrated ivy.
I draw a round in the breath
of the early mirror;
and so I vary the chore of checking
up on myself, with all
these beauty aids.
Pre-breakfast
never grows tedious by ecstasy,
red-cheeked and active, I
contingency plan:

a spot on the chin, not a dimple
but a plain kitchen spot: an apple a day.
A little flab on the waist,
corsetting of course, and ribbons to pull tight
unbearably, dear, in bright colours.
Then hair straggles, I think of
thin bone scratchy gypsy combs.
I think of her minutely

I stare in, seeing her blank line,
I call, mirror, mirror
narrowing my eyes
like a renowned painter laying in the first stroke.

Leda and Leonardo the swan

Leda, the inside out lady of the swan
    wants to knuckle the cold
rotter who fluttered her to bed.

Caught in the infinite wiggle
in a mesmerization of paint
      here she is, propped in her voluptuous stay
                  maddened
for all who like a good sex object
shielding her feathered friend.

His beak pinches her demonstrable little
breasts, quacking all mine
      her plump pubic mound pretty and public
her eyes abashed
how she blushes, the mystery!
      my corrected darling!

The silent curly face
carries on talking backwards to the wall
no   no   no   no.

Lament for the child

The little girl instinctively
makes things nice
bedding her dolls down
the lion with its plastic muzzle off
the tailless squirrel,
her father eats like a chimpanzee
smacking his lips at the table
with pears and peaches.

The white doll and the black
each with set upraised ghoulish lip
stiff in their shoebox lie,
she has this instinct
this capacity, for making things nice –
for method,

and her mother offers cotton and rags
and plumes in with scraps
of silver satin, turquoise taffeta
lace ripped off old bedwraps
feathers from felt hats
found on a dirty shelf.

Her father leaves, but her mother
devises cut-up dolls' blankets, cut-up sheets
dolls' insecure dresses
squares for minute fraying scarves
which she won't offer to stitch because certainly
she doesn't want to.

And now at last the new parent surveys
her row of mummies
swathed, nestling, boxed, unreturning
and she is tender, and capacious
with love; and making things nice.

In memory, 1978

I want to lament the princess who was killed
gunned down by the henchmen of her grandfather
     in the main square of Jeddah.
She was a princess so she was gunned,
ordinary women are stoned to death for adultery,
their lovers lose their heads, which is to
     teach other men not to.
For the women the lorry reverses into the square
     tips out a pile of ordinary stones
which at sunset are picked out by the faithful
under the adjuration of a holy man
they being all men, the adulteress is made to
     stand upright inside a sack,
they throw the stones at her till the sack falls
     over, and go on till she dies.

When the sun sets, here the crescent
     rises – she sees neither,
having been a believer all her life, done
everything dutifully but one thing:
which was to remain behind her black seven veils
     every living moment: to
take her flesh to sackcloth from birth
     to death: to
keep their eyes clean for God, and
his rigid kings and small fathers on earth:
     she salaams down
onto, dear God, well-trodden ground.

The long-haired woman

Burning out my throat
with the mildest cigarettes
listening from woman to woman
from house to pub to flat to cafe to house
    on the phone
to the next woman
with her blue eyes
and her thin breasts that I want to
    talk to as well
and her print-inked fingers
who reminds me of her own poem
of the woman with long hair met on a street
    (her hair floats, though in our backwaters)
and listening, and doing what I think's
    called gossiping
but it's not like that to me
more of a race: like a racehorse
where I pull back and let go, pull back
    and let go
and we racehorses all run together
headed into the wind
a great fatigue
but not mildewing and rotting and watching.

The bath

This dark of which I am the face,
this cave beach my canoe finger explores,
stretched and ribbed like ship spars

or this cavemouth of water or blood,
swamped

drifting anemones out
from my womb to sea,
the lost fronds of a cradle unwound

a gentle loss,
my finger winds a tiny curl of my leaving

– softhead
birthing myself in bathwater –

How she feared for him

Her son descended the powdered ocean
through the pierced planes
      of the half dense half green sea
his face washed well, which it never was
a lead two inch diver in his vast bath
head erect, knees, feet together
dropping like a lost policeman
freely, soberly and soundless
sacrificial and vertical
down to the water bottom.

She waved to her son falling
through the pierced planes of the sobersides sea
the smile on his apply cheek
split – split to a look of horror
through the green attic just below the surface
daylit, he sank through to the main
      mansion of the gulf.

She assumed he'd rise   three times
and come out
but he did not
      it was murder in the dark.

She saw him pass like a sliderule
      to the ocean cellar
her hands she found pasted palm to palm
so she couldn't dive even as a gesture
she wrenched her heart like an anemone
his stilled baby's blood on her hands –
his wrinkled and dwarfed look
intensely pleading his mother
      then shot of life.

Descending like a two inch lead diver
head erect, knees and feet together
like a lost policeman
going down to her crime.

Circe

Circe, queen of the foreign land
outside the mouth of the known sea
sits in her summer villa
walks on the garden shore.
The wind purrs at her heels
the following wind of that place.

She is a green fingered woman
making fruit in a wet valley
corn from a bare hill,
kids and lambs on the flanks of the ocean
under the piled colossi of hiding clouds.
The gentle breasted farmer –
pig woman, caster of spells!

No-one has seen her for sure,
on the lost ship their
ears prick with horror
a lamb's bleat or a pig's grunt through
the cracked storm
this may be Circe
or this may.

I cannot have mercy, only knowledge
the goddess sings at her loom
and makes poison as we make coffee.
There are alders by the landing stage
and lambs, and temples.

A long time later came Odysseus,
his men ran snorting under her wand
but he knew her
he scuttled her cauldron.

The witch had children,
he liked her charms for a while
then tired,
unscrambled his men and left
for his dour home, his proper
wife and her lack of a rival wand.

I cannot have mercy, only knowledge –
he told Circe, this girl
of the ports
she said goodbye and told him
how to go.
She may have cried, but a goddess
or a witch, the woman of quiet
breasts, the taloned,
the blue sea
won't cry long.

Atlantic seals

Their cough floats up the hollow hole
heatwave converse
aching, indulgent:
eyes, they say, that pop
with wisdom, of the unchangeable
slug princes – their small
Ruritania of the rocks
down there
propped in the thin boom of waves
a court of voices.

Queen Clytemnestra

Part One

They say this is her tomb,
Queen Clytemnestra of the fortress of Mycenae,
fronting the limey plain of Argos
where oxen plough
and cars proceed to Corinth and to Athens.

Then her body has regained her soul,
there being no sign of her;
the hot cell is dusty and barred off,
laid with tribute of coke bottles.

Clytemnestra, queen of the grand absurd name,
Clytie in her nightie,
the big bosom pushing through the frills
as she drowns the hero in his bath,
queen of the long claws,
the bearded virago;

and you took your lover – took him!
little lisping Aegisthus,
and were married in Agamemnon's blood and bathwater.

If you had behaved yourself,
you would be beautiful now and adorned.
Orestes would have remembered you
kindly to his grandchildren
and even Electra grown up less cross.
Your face should have been
pale, calm, oval,
tender,
your hair neatly ringletted
instead of this viperous mess,
as black as the old witch Medea's.
And black your heart and eyes, Clytemnestra,
black queen of the hill, king killer,

throne grabber,
open-thighed blasphemer,
she who would be king.

Certainly he left you regent
and you and your boyfriend made the most of it
– you didn't stay faithful long,
only a couple of years out of the ten
and Aegisthus was one in a long daisy-chain –
yes, between you extorting every last jar,
the grape wagons lumbering for your carousals
and when Agamemnon landed at last,
in good health but sick of ships and tents
and eager for his house and to deal justice
and rule in one place, and for you
whom he still imagined slender,
your long lids painted blue,
cobra bracelets on your arm,
and Electra his last daughter
– simply couldn't imagine her grown-up –

well, he was in pretty good shape,
stout-necked, thick-haired, almost the
son of the minotaur in chest measurement,
and he wasn't stupid, he'd kept
the Greeks together in the Trojan bogs
for a decade, for all their tantrums
and home sickness; moreover stayed top cat.

You met him at the head of the path
under the great stone lintel:
welcome, my lord, welcome home,
having told Aegisthus to take a short walk.
Agamemnon clutched you
(you were more of a handful than he remembered
and your eyeshadow was green now).
Then there were compliments and civic speeches
and then a banquet. He got pissed
of course. And you

waited offstage cool as a winejar,
seeing him slouched in his chair
and calling for hot water.

This is Agamemnon splashing in the tub
in the sun, guffawing, his arms and back
covered with war bites,
his hands calloused as they grab for you.
How neatly you unpicked the seam of his head
with the bronze needle of his own axe
– didn't you think of younger days,
how he savaged you with love
and your arse rose and you sank together
and you, the young queen, wrapped in your hair,
groaned as he touched the spring of your heart
– you blocked that off, letting
the blood pool out into water
and splash, as he twists, downhill
through the baked cisterns.

Then all would have gone on before,
Aegisthus returning with a nice healthy look
and you, Clytemnestra double crowned at last!

But Electra, whose ideas of fatherhood
over ten years had expanded into the cosmos,
seeing the sodden flesh, cried in a corner
and wouldn't come to dinner;
no use not eating, said the queen,
what's done can't be undone,
but she had forgotten her son Orestes
the hero. He stroked his mother with his blade
and Electra laughed like crazy.
Then the house was empty.

Later the Dorians burned the fort.
Maybe they found the bones of the usurper
and stole her gravegoods,
stripping the old finger bones of their rings

and the masked skull of its gold,
kicking the skeleton into the bushes:
a pile of whore's rubbish.

Part Two

In Aulis before the great war,
before I died
– what do I care for my bones?
Let the Dorians, the Romans, the Turks
and the visiting professors
pick them over, decide which are mine,
which are the servant's
or the dog's
– my living face needed no mask –

In Aulis before the war
the fleets were gathered, and the sea was calm.
Troy had stolen the wind.
Miles eastward Helen laughed in Asia
and here Menelaus raged; the sea stayed still,
the sky stretched to the gods.
My husband the king Agamemnon counted
the allied ships;
dusk after dusk men slipped home
and the count dwindled.
So he announced, with the priests
of the sacred grove there: a sacrifice,
that was the answer.
Poseidon earthshaker needed a carrot,
a bribe to bounce them over to Troy
(he put it less crudely, or
more pompously)
a carrot: a human sacrifice.
The generals clapped, we all smiled with relief
– a few wrinkled their noses, but that was
to show the king uncouth and oldfashioned,
in fact they all did it in emergencies,
it always soothed the god –

as for me I wanted to get home
and see to Mycenae,
the leavetaking was getting embarrassing
and the nightly drinking parties
with their boasts and oaths by every god
to be a man at Troy
bored me.

Even Iphigenia, chasing crabs in the pools, was
bored of the grown-up treat,
seeing the navy sail, and wanted home:
romantic twelve year old, crying for Menelaus
and for her beautiful aunt, abducted!

Iphigenia my eldest sits in my lap
in the evening, talking.
I brush back her hair and kiss her shoulders,
she wriggles and smiles, don't do that,
kisses me with a soft mouth
as when a baby she kissed my breasts
and sucked and stared at me with large eyes –
now goes to her father's quarters
for she likes that flat shaggy chest
in a way I do not.

I think of how at her age
I galloped a horse in my father's field.
Now I ride in a litter and
hide my mouth in my cloak
but they know the black eyes of Clytemnestra.

I feel the skin of my daughter, like potpourri,
overnight the nipples flowered,
sweet orchids, pushing. I could have placed
my mouth over each. How soft they seemed.
You were pleased when you noticed,
then displeased. I teased that soon
you'd be grown and off my hands.
You sulked and forgot and ran to the shore.

My Iphigenia, it was a cold shore
you never deserved,
wild anchorage for your running heels.
Over the years after, at Mycenae
I saw you, graveless,
your ashes fed to Poseidon,
small handful of my daughter,
plump and twelve years old,
whose body they burned,
the princess Iphigenia,
having burst your heart with a dagger
at the king's nod.

You fool, he conned you,
your father, with the lust of a pure death
and the thanks of Greece.
Would he have killed Orestes
if the god had wanted? You,
Iphigenia, were dispensable
holy fodder, bred for a blood object
and I, I bore you and fed you
and played with your toes
and taught you letters, and to sing,
and laughed as you ran
shrieking through the house,
just for that –

You laughed at my wailing
and sang upward in the trance
of this giving
and layed on the stone in the grove,
your eyes rolled backwards, Iphigenia the adored,
and your father nodded
and they kissed your infant bones.

In the years after, I swore,
over and over, not to forget it,
nor who did it.

That was at night . . .
in the day Mycenae throve,
free of the bad temper of soldiers.
We guarded the villages
and they fed us:
wheat, oil, wine, skins, meat.
We lorded a land of dairies,
the herds gave us milk,
we laid in funds of mountain bees:
in our larders
rows of vases of honey.
The farmers respected me
and my head for figures,
quicker than Agamemnon's, who in peacetime
spent his nights fuddled
and the days hunting.
My policy was hard but consistent
and there was peace
and settled trade with Tyryns, Argos and further.
I minted my people peace
and they bred me honey, my queen bee days.

As for the Greek army
our young men sailed east each year
and by the same ships returned old men,
limbless, one-eyed, their skin
discoloured with huge scars.
They sat in my bright hall and mumbled of heroes,
something about Achilles or the Trojan Hector
or that Agamemnon had fought like a bear
in some skirmish or other
and of his dozen concubines,
pretty young barbarians . . .
they shut their mouths and went out to the sun
but my nightmare spoke.

One spring Orestes, in full armour, left for Troy.

I took Aegisthus to warm me,
he watched me wind and thread my hair
in the old Cretan way,
his broad hands coaxed my hips,
at nights he slept in the crook of my shoulder,
his nose rubbing my breast and
I pulled his curls and stared
at the mountains;
he was twenty,
he did not interfere with business.

I haven't mentioned Electra – what
can I say?
Somewhere in the house she played, I suppose,
if Electra ever played.

Well, I come of a narrow race of women
and Agamemnon was not exactly small.
Of all my births, hers was the worst,
I suffered with her and she with me, I suppose,
a crying, crying baby.
I gave her to a wet nurse and preferred Iphigenia.
After Aulis I did not wish to see her.

Spring in, autumn out, Troy stood
like a brass hill, like one of ours:
except for the drain of boys, younger
and younger, we almost forgot that
half Greece was abroad
(some of the old timers in the end
that came back hardly knew what soil this was
and talked queer Greek).
Then the hill split, Troy fell,
a footsoldier lugged Priam by the beard
and spat at him dying;
six weeks later I heard of it.
We all heard. Electra in the silence
spoke, my father is coming home,

she looked at me across the table,
her eyes were stone black.

In fact it was autumn when they came,
lime-trees sprinkled their chariots and
swallows dithered over the field
still between his dust and my city.

All through the ceremony, the feast, his belches,
Troy had not improved his manners –
the street mayhem, handgripping
with the old professionalism,
his bellowing at the girls showering
flowers from the windows, for whom
he was brand new,
his wild men roaring,
I saw how:
the sea flows down and up, up and down
and ashes do not rest,
therefore downhill, downhill,
in water and blood I sent him to find her.

After he was dead I retched,
throwing up my mess to join the one at my feet
and laughed with tears in my eyes
and shook as after an illness.
I turned. Electra stood
in the cunning shadow of the mountain
green-faced with sick. I
passed her.

Orestes had not returned,
presumed dead or missing.
I married Aegisthus; that
went against the grain
but my council demanded a king
to ease its conscience:
we were not in Amazon country,
the King is dead – long live the King.

We buried Agamemnon with the correct supplies,
with silver and lapis lazuli and
ivories, and a hunting dog or two
and clothes, and weapons.
And we spread lies.
Electra kept to her quarters,
said to be sick or
in mourning.
The streets were dead quiet.

That winter was unusually cold;
once, hailstones cut the bay at Navplion
and the hills froze.
I worked at my accounts
and kept quiet,
dissuading the idiot Aegisthus
from the splended idea of thanksgiving games.
I sent him to the hills for boar
and paced the throne room
clutching myself for cold:
time for Mycenae, time.

He brought back twelve tusked monsters
slung between spears from stumpy legs.
I pinched his cheek and ran my face
between the muscles of his thighs,
licking, and calling him
little hunter most excellent and –
my Ganymede, and
the deerhide sprang back and
there stood my son.
I laughed; the two boys
stared at each other,
Aegisthus grabbed for his dagger too late,
Orestes said, mother,
I stared at him; he had thickened and scarred,
I couldn't see his eyes under the crest,
his hair was darker brown, greasy, long,
I was thinking it needed a wash
when he threw the spear.

Downhill   downhill
the combs from my hair clatter, my citadel breaks.
Electra, I thank you,
I am always repaid in ashes,
for loving, for hating, for killing, for giving,
for wrecking and for building
to my glory and to the old glory of these plains
and these flocks and these uplands,
I am paid in ashes.
You and I shared once: our vomit.
Electra, whose bones must be somewhere around
under the road or the car-park
or the new motorway, or
gone deep under the masonry,
Electra, we are both graveless,
we share twice,
be quiet now and join your sister.

At home

I can't let the dear plants die,
now can I, dear, said the
old lady, digging her toy fork
into the window-box as if
for potatoes. The
petunias nodded.
I don't really like gardening,
she added. I don't much
like my budgie either, she added,
his name is Sam. I'd prefer
to be in a comatose state than
clean Sam out, and it's a strain
making polite conversation, he
likes to talk. D'you like him?
The Social Worker brought him in
to keep me sentient and my
faculties critical. Now, dear,
isn't it time for your bus?

Those upright men

I heard of a tribe where the men
                    held their erections all their lives,
like rhino horns: each
his own mascot before the main regiment of the body,
gorgeous trophies
                    painful to bump.

How was it done? by jockstraps
                              loincloths de luxe
with withies?

            by suggestion?
the curves of their own country as they hunted,
the round waterhole, the swollenness of coconuts
the plump streams
                    coiling and juicing from the buttocks
                    of herbaceous mountains?

Were their dreams never dry?
                    love men of endless fervor
or were they the red-eyed servants of their women,
hot and cold for endless foreplay?
or were they workers, exploited, forklifting their semen
                    under stern state frottage,
for there were few men in their nation:
                              in numbers not large.

Or was it just   virilismus
            a muscular kink?

They painted themselves, for ceremonial
in colour contrasts of rising bands of pigments
                              of riverbank clay
            red, white and blue.

                    Those upright men
I believe, wore their cocks instead of ties
                                    or truths
or guns;
                                    or socks.

Ruminations of Red Riding Hood

There is a time for the wolf
       and I am a wise woman
I can tell you: there is a time
       for that scarlet leer.

     *   *   *

 Only in a wood with bunny rabbits
and violets and Disney birds
thyroidal eye of joy, flipping and singing
head cocked from tree-branch, the sun out
altogether now, it was like that when
        I went to see my granny;
 after all he might have been
just a simple friendly soul, not a wolf
or if a wolf, a kindly converted
seen the error of his ways, ardent religious
 love to all, flower behind his sloping ear

but when he launched at me
        nightdress rearing
the frilled and floral night-cap stood off
       like a parachute
and his narrow single-boned face (scrunched
        to a scimitar)
filled granny's squeaky little bedroom
       and the glass animals
fell flat on the bookcase and the Doulton ladies'
heads and fluted petticoats rolled here, there
      and everywhere

and granny began to sing oh so softly
in the din, and muffled: and I shrieked
for the woodman who was kipping under a beech
    when he should have been sitting
up and listening for screams and all alert
for carnage and to come quick, but he
had dematerialized; and it was then
    I saw my mistake
                    and understood:

there is a time for the wolf
there always comes a time
and I am not a very wise woman,
                    there is a time
                    for that red morsel
for the matchless excruciating teeth
the appetite unhindered
                    of the eaten person and the eater
                    the scalding wolf;

in the middle of the pupil of the adult eye
among the figurines
the wolf.

               *   *   *

Persephone

Each round table has a red shade;
                              they dim the lights
and spin the diamonds of the globe for dancing.
Madame eats her dinner underground,
                                      multicoloured.
Over her crêpe-de-chine shoulder
                    the large face of Hades
is discernible, all gloom and glum
and as hot as mustard in the dark.

Overground, Demeter paces impatiently,
poking at rabbit-holes with her gardener's hoe,
she'd rake back miles of earth:
                    she's out too late.
Above her, the moon's in fruit and silver,
that's no comfort; when new mists bear
in over low ground
                    Persephone's gone.

2

Mother, you don't know anything
                    about this place,
you live overground.
None of the colours, browns and blues
                    and greens of the early fields
hurt my eyes, and when I was my mother's girl
I was happy in corn and sorrel and clover.
I knew your fingers and your breath
                    could grow anything
and everything was nourished by you.
You taught me
          petal, stem and stamen of the lily

and how its waxed bulb
                    roots in the damp earth.
Later on I saw the kick of the wind
                    in the belly of the forest
and you sowed on below, your back firm,
the seed tossed over your shoulder
and me idling behind,
                    merely thinking of poppies.

3

In his garden
        before the irises of my eyes expanded
I grazed my hands on the trunks of poplars
too dark to see. The leaves curled
                            like wax.
The hothouses steamed with fruit,
                        not your sort.
I was crying aloud, but more and more hungry
                        . . . hear me now
then I ate the seeds.
The red pomegranate dampened and consoled my lips
and the irises of my eyes expanded.

How we dance, here, in slow time
                    under the globe.

4

I'm tired.
        It's been a long time, the night
and I've settled my thirst for a while.
He moves round
            the light filtering room
with his sleeves rolled back,
                    clearing.
Shall I come up and see you
Demeter, my starved and daughterless,
only a visit, for I've
                a queenship of my own
coloured hard.

45

I take the unmanageable darkness
                           since I can rule it.
On those terms you'll kiss me –
Oh mother, unveil the beloved earth again
                           when I come.

For my daughter

Don't be in a hurry, Miranda . . .
the old mother, you know,
remembers herself at your age,
sixteen is it, well I,
well you are too beautiful, time
to leave . . . ?
Don't be in a hurry,
my smouldering eye-liner.
Keep your mane twirled round you.

As for those well formed
fishnet calves
pedalling to school
out of black suede
fringed high-heeled ankle boots
– to display
or disown? But that's a difficulty
you've got taped. Oh
nobody whistles, you say
scornfully when I wonder.
Clearly, you measured the world?

You prowl the house
like a crusader's queen, black
eyebrowed. The crusader herself,
my mail-fisted beauty . . .
Well, on your way then:
more strategy than I had.
You make me remember bad years, the
loss of Jerusalem.
Hurry, Miranda . . .

Wait   wait.

49

A woman making advances publicly

A woman making advances publicly
twin spots of rouge
her chin quivers
yeast mask she took
for freshness, and forgot
to wipe off, before the door.
So gay her brave
eyes and the whites, like a dog,
upturned;
twin rouge, she's bright gaunt
thirty-nine, like me.
Where from this crow, dredged
up so, this whore, to scare?
Times lost, of the bright lined smiles,
the timid skull
X-rayed straight out.
Where from, my father,
learned and rapt father,
when, knee high to a grasshopper
I stood by your leg,
you on the lawn bench, long
time past, reading
a holy book,
I standing in my best dress
shy into my mother's camera.
I did not look so strange.

Ava Gardner in the film *Earthquake*

Expensive, her throat
the white of a fattened column.
Alcoholic. Weeping. If she hadn't started
the day in L.A. that way:
evil would have stayed put
underground. Envies unfold
from her soured silk. The city
dives upward on her malice.
Scorned by Charlton husband, she
rifts the land. And his
towers crumple.

When the dam breaks
there Ava must die: her power
drowns even her. Heston hero
she takes, for his cold
blood. Dead the stately hairy
engineer, lost by her
in dirt of tunnels below
his towers: by this long-lidded
ageing. She
should have constrained it,
her reaching throat.

Ava ageing baby,
beforehand
you kept nagging:
you swayed out warning
(don't pick up that secretary).
You shook the towers.
Not to rush ladders, electric
typewriters, glass bowls
of flowers, cabinets of Scotch
and safes to the sky.
No way to soar, if I'm to lie
underfoot and hold.

Sadly gurgled Charlton,
acknowledging this with muddy
ghost of
sight, before lost
in the opened wounds and come
down and into earth again
to be with you
as man with wife.

At the National Gallery

A flow of people looking.
The baby sucks at its mother's breasts.
One tucked away, one full, the
nipple a guava fruit – dark and ready.
The mother sitting in the National Gallery
on a black-buttoned seat, in
an unzipped anorak, the baby slung,
could be copying the
madonna she herself gazes at and drinks in,
over the way: a limpid, tidy
countenance on the wall there, her own
small teat held neatly with a crystal
cherry ending for the Christ Child Jesus
to nibble, who blesses us all.

The Keeper finds the mother of the guava
breast, and with a flurried, frowning, jerking
– the public don't want to see that sort of thing here
– orders to take herself off, and baby and
breast, and zip it in quick. The
baby stops and cries, furious. Eyes flow past.
The mother feeds it again, looking at the wall.

Wrap it up – the Keeper
sees the broad breast, giving food
under his hand, so near he could stroke the skin.
– D'you want to make an exhibition of yourself?
He pulls her. She backs to the wall.
The Madonna of the Guava
(hung near the much loved
Madonna of the Cherry) is a fine recently
acquired picture attributed to.
Experts have judged it lifelike, for example in the
bluish pores of the nipple outstretched to the

lips of the child, still crying. It
now hangs in the National Gallery
– streams of people –
as part of the permanent collection.

The Pope at Dublin Airport, 1979

Oh the relief of the children!
After the barrier rows of the priests
each razored and batter skinned face
asymmetrical, pressured with
spectacle jammed on bull brow by brow
lined – body versus soul
jarring like bouncers, night issue
by issue –
But the relief of the children!

Oh the smiling of the mothers!
Whose dresses blow in the wind. And they hold
the beloveds up to the broad
Pope's delighted grin. At something simple –
simply to suffer – no jarring – but (for him) –
more of the little children
to live and die in Christ, in Ireland
in Asia, in Latin America.
Oh the blessed wombs of the mothers!

Oh the especial blessing of the Papa!
His grin that takes them – soft children
among the ridged men – And in
Bolivia Christian souls dig filth and tin
and die short – now may more replace them
to dig out more tin, to fly the Papa Pope
Father round the world, with God's love, in.
This is the smile, at Dublin.
Addressed to men, women and children.

The horses of instruction, the tigers of wrath

– from Blake's Proverbs of Hell

The horses of instruction
tell slowly forward
under the gables of Europe, of Asia, of Africa.
Along streets of cobble or mud or tarmac
the horses pull with their sedate flanks
wagons of detritus,
a grandfather clock that can
tell the hours by an antique chime.
It stands crooked among saucepans and children.
This is the commentary of the horses.
Their heavy necks strain
in a direction given by a driver
who strains with lassitude to exit
somewhere, for somewhere.

This is the wrath of the tiger.
A mouth's shout, private and momentary.
The disputations on the forking paths, and
the huzzahings in the wider alleys
confronting the glass shields.
Stones are the wrath, the articulate fist in the face.
Bullets are the wrath, the fist on the table.
It is not the day for any of this
or even the mere savagery of a beast.
The razed jungle prefers empires
of glitter, and the
stainless thermo-nuclear device.
Nevertheless stones will be the wrath,
bullets will be the wrath. Listen
to the makers of true words,
this is the desperate hour
of our speaking.
Words we speak. We remember.
Our words are raised up over the patient
horse of the world: we remember.

There is the driver who has no road.
In the name of the already dead,
put down your toy that
occupies the earth,
your spinning, symmetric and burning toy,
you death makers, you device makers.

for Hiroshima Day 1981

Playing water polo in Angola

in the words of an ex-South African
mercenary, 32 Battalion, reported Feb '81

Sometimes you do it to the children
to make the adults talk.
We wanted to know what was going on.
We wanted to make his mother talk.

So we tied him up like a chicken,
wrists and ankles behind his back.
We put him in this kind of dam.
We pushed him about and let him sink.

We played this water-polo with him.
Every so often we took him out.
He wouldn't cry, he just wet himself.
The mother didn't tell us anything.

In the end we just left him in.
Some of our guys get very involved:
that's going too far and I don't enjoy it,
I just don't like that sort of thing.

Cinderella

I must take a grip on myself
sitting in cinders, I to myself.
This ball, I never wanted to go.
Their silky eyelids, I'll not care.

The moon passes the basement window
like a sugar mouse nosing
for pie in the sky. For ever
ash lines my throat; I'll not mind.

Here is the castle, we have come to.
Peacocks and peahens promenade
backwards and forwards on moon
strewn paths, rustling and shrieking.

Hey prince, prince, now you
brighten. Lickspit your natty
moustache, your strawberry lips to
wet mine, your curved finger

to pull me, giggling in my best
my lovely rags, dizzy with dancing,
my waist hot with turning.
Their silky eyelids baste red.

And having scoured what I wanted,
thwarted lust, jealousy and fury,
I left them all to the pieces –
any brittle idea they could find.

Fire

Neither of us wanted
this flame to run the street.
We held careful, dry torches
and only eyed each other a little.

This twin flame, this
wall. My heartbeat
shivers before the increasing circle,
my breath packs into gasps.

Gently scoring the track around, around,
you hardly knew I was
your last colour, a flicker –
I appeared and fired up changeably.

Now I am nearly made into
your firelight; therefore
wait, explain gently – my mouth
faints to carry your fire.

Uncollected (1977–1982)

Two old Fabians watch Conference

prod the box, Albert
the Conference is on this afternoon
we're stricken deer, and slow
                        and sunlight dapples
our greenhouse
have you noticed, Albert, how our
                        geraniums' petals'
crimson blows?

the doctor tells me I need sun for
                        my shoulders
sun, like embrocation, I wish we had
                        a policy for sun
this is a lovely debate
this quiet man knows about incomes related pensions
I like his eyes, and child allowances
his boyish downfalling serious hair

dearest, d'you understand about inflation, no
                        but really
this one I can't follow
is it his accent or my hearing
sometimes our fellow workers are very strange
remember, Albert, the time you
                        struck, or meant to
such a peaceful picket . . . these miners
                        are so big

Albert, isn't it odd the way our
                        geraniums' petals
return and go
how the green buds split into red
and then they rot
unpleasant, really

see that raven haired woman talking
talking her head off, at the mike
I think she's quite right
look, the Chairman's lit up a small red bulb
                    to stop her

Albert, pull up your chair, dearest
                    sitting there
all tangled in clematis – you're asleep
I knew it. dearest, awake
                    the cat's in your seedling
and go now to our kitchen and make us tea

Limb of God

My father: a long tadpole,
a baby's first lean shape.
He does breast stroke, to keep
immortal, in the dew.

Early one May morning
he adds up minuscule lengths.
Back and forth the pull of
retired biceps and wavy shins.

Dew flashes clear pendants
from the temple roof, and slops
from the bubbly sheet, the
pool cover that catches leaves –

wound back now by my
mother; she knows everything.
There he blows, that
white-skinned limb of God,

heating the water with puffs.
Once out, he sneezes and sneezes,
raucous as the cow's cough
beyond, in the dew-chained meadow.

My mother swims in her bath hat.
He dances with a towel,
hobbledehoy at the heater
under the pearly gable.

The old man dying

– in memory of Andromache and Constantine Kazantzis

The old woman sits with drooping mouth
waiting for the old man
to live again.
He lies in his red wing armchair,
brocade, flustered and tatty.
His sighs are regular and swell
to moans.
Don't listen to him, he's putting it on.
And she turns him
and feeds him on baby foods.
When his brain swings back
a cell at a time, at twilight
for ten minutes before his bedtime,
her cynic's face goes tender:
eyes under the hooded chalky lids
brighten.
Daddy is good today. He's better. See!
He turns his bald head on its dewlap
like a tortoise, nosing
for sun. Later he sleeps.
She wipes the dribble from his lips
and heaving and panting, corseted, small,
she carefully beds him for the night.
All night she patchily sleeps,
her thick back aches, and
she listens for his moans, and for the change
of breath, the elusive and dreadful
departure.

A custom

Daughters are used as hacks
drooping along side lanes
They have soft affectionate tucked in chins
They feel they get any old rider.

'Tell him' exclaim the mothers
flinging up their rounded arms in their prime
of success, which seems endless
not least to their daughters.

'Tell him!' In their seventies
the mothers are still at it, seductive
and pink-cheeked, 'he's absolutely . . .'
and the daughters obey.

Drooping along to the 'him'
and telling him . . . 'her favourite man!'
And he returns, via this pale faced
lady, a note of cheeky adulation.

from
Let's Pretend (1984)

The nurse's sorrow

He is the old year,
you look at his sharp chin,
his shrivelled paunch like
a crabapple tightly
stranded in cold
wet brown grass.
He's as docile as a
fieldmouse, no idea
of enmity, just to be
friendly. Beware him.
He'll tie you in grass
like swaddling
          because

he'd love a child,
he'll rock anybody walking.
All the livelong day. But
the flowers on the
open hill are
blowing harder than he tells –
The sea is minstrel blue,
it falls down hundreds of feet
it rises up, it
lifts its arm, it
with a whirr fans the blank
chalk face, the cliff
hefts up its white bodiless face
on pinions.

All valley here, he says;
he clogs with violets
under the hedge.
All starlit night he
whispers the dawn chorus
to pacify his babe
(who is ineffably angry)

and to bring the promise
of a lovely day.
                        Isn't it

the cold heart
who'll tread down such kind
sorrow of the nurse?
Will you hush
in his cradle?
Here is
the bony frame: its
shadow, to
and fro on the grass.
                      O angry babe.

A Sussex lady

Channel clouds darken the flint farm.
They pass like long vehicles
over the dove cotes, over
the family of high-necked swans.

Remember the mermaid-tail roofs
and the black-eyed chapel
of Lewes, like a duck
on a bank between the cars.
Remember the slur of the Ouse
towards and away from a deep
                              and obedient pond,
netted by road, wire, pole.
You can see the pure sports cars
seed in the valley
like lilies; from Beddingham Beacon.

I keep my voice up.
I speak from a vigorous throat.
My heart
misses a beat sometimes, but not
in the garden.
Nasturtiums grow like the faces
of my daughters,
                      quiet rioters.
They are green and weak
and go everywhere.

Mr Tanner is cutting down
his silvery weeping willow tree.
I drink from a Jubilee mug,
on yellowy green tweed
knees, my preferred tea.

And I watch the last sun go down
behind the elms.
The rooks are displaced yearly
onto lower,
less imperial,
less heartfelt trees.

I mean, the backwater
city of my head,
the locked up towers –
I have withdrawn my bowmen
and abandoned the flowery
                          maypole wards
for the squalor hits below the waist.

I walk the blue farmlands of the downs.
A kindly labrador nurses my heel.
There is the evening news
                          coming from the sea
in the swelling mist.
I run my finger along my arm, for dust.

Silver hands

Shielding my ego,
it's a tiny ego but monstrous,
from her critical eyes
though she looks away

to a horizon of pale blue
hills and ideal waves
glimmer of waves
at evening.

She looks avaunt but
I know what she thinks
(I think) back through
tread of her ideal

to where my activities –
like the soil that is
full of ants, running and
apparently running, this way

and that – to where my
queenship burrows in
and disturbs the repose of
the matron, the madonna, the mother

the mother of the family –
What can I tell the great
world, I have no
silver hands, no fame.

At Mrs Leigh's

Under the tinned rhubarb sky
it's dark in Shepherd's Bush.
Tubes on the track purr through
and wind through the closed market
burrs down to my gas fire.

Upstairs they're playing guitar wisps
and gentle gestures. Their shoes
squeak and pinch and tumble
overhead. They visit the loo
as the train purrs; and the pipes sing

against the great soft roar beyond
the walled garden. In that
dark orange clouded garden
in a homemade rubberised pond
five fish lie, of Mrs Leigh.

The humble beer

The humble beer at my right hand,
the fire a bar before my toe,
the television square ahead,
the sofa yielding to my rear,
the kettle pouting on the stove.

The sheriff switching smoking guns,
the tender chop upon the plate,
the fork to left, the knife to right.
The sheriff scolds the fiery whore,
the kettle pouting on the stove.

The bashful sheriff eyes the whore,
the knife and fork upon the chop,
the humble beer leaves little dregs,
the whore and sheriff ponder life,
the kettle whispers on the stove.

The sofa emanates a doze,
the fire recirculates my toes,
the whore and sheriff lose their clothes,
the tender chop inside me goes,
the kettle slumbers on the stove.

The doorman

The doorman dreams of the door.
His hat is blue, braided
with hotel gold.
Today he opened the door
sometimes one way,
sometimes the other
with a smile apparent under
his moustache.
The double doors split before the guests
who sailed out or lapped home.
He moved before or behind
his grave moustache turning upwards
like a black November leaf.
He enlarged the door space fully
to give passage to the rapid guests.
In bed, to sleep, he counts
up the reversing swish.
One pull inwards, one pull outwards,
two inwards, two outwards
till he ebbs on a hoovered carpet
printed with whirlpools,
then flows to, on steel pivots
and sleeps and snores.

In the dream, his
shoulders are solid ice,
his hat wheels around lightly,
his teeth are huge glass panels
inside
that swing to, and grind
and swing back.

A thatcher

A thatcher is someone who makes a roof
or used to, when things were quieter,
was someone who sheltered people
from the rain, when things were quieter.
A thatcher took folks from the wind
and layered the skin of a human weather.
Now a thatcher exposes the dwellers,
rips off the roof in the skinning wind,
hurls down the roof on the dwellers,
who for cover snatch at the straws
the roof-maker rains
on their rainwashed heads ruthlessly
and in their teeth and in their eyes
like a war
that the thatcher unnaturally makes
on the dwellers. And the luckier,
snatching more straw cover of the undoing
thatch, despise the unluckier, the colder ones,
so that some see but many don't
or do see but not why, and think it
the way of a brave wise thatcher
that their fellows are icy and cold
in an inhuman country.

The ending we are projected

It denudes all partings,
all lovers whose fingers
ladder together, walking towards
the desert field,
all children who shout for the parent
who recedes through the wood
of scraped trees,
all parents who watch
their children leaf upwards
into outer air.

It demeans all who are old
and break breath like stones
to keep breath till breath breaks.
Draw curtain or not,
it means the blackening of the room.

We are used to going away,
trained to its regular sound
as regular as the heart
in its single casing.
We are handed out at birth
onto two full breasts, one pleasure,
one grief, and grow between both.
But this projected parting
rejects all offers,
fouls flow,
poisons our mouths.
Childish or old,
our goodbyes are made mad.

Our goings are tinged
and sucked into its rearing aura
where a one-eye gropes out –
It boils up dust, from which nothing.
It spits out a process of nothing

and us the projected grist. We must
not let our griefs, our parted natures
be so annulled, so further emended;
we are ironclad and clouded over
to denuded and sour
dust and nothing.

for Hiroshima day, 1983

Anna Akhmatova

Who with a reserved voice
spoke for dead
millions. Who appointed herself.
Who prepared

with Fear and the Muse
standing watch by turn.
To speak the acknowledgement.

And incredible to me
the poet given and by herself
such valid graces, such statue

bronze-lidded by the Neva
where prison doves coo.
The killed voices, flying up, out,
always.

On the coast

1

On the coast
we do not float far from
our own concerns,
cutting the melons six ways
for breakfast at nine and twelve.

The children in the swimming pool
float there, legs
interwoven like whiskery
prawns, in unnatural blue.
Yesterday all day too.

And Chloe's hair
begins to change its do:
straight honey lines.
She tips her nose out,
flickers her frogskin eyes.

The boys below
chat unnatural science
over fetta and marmalade.
In the bay
a shark is felt to heel and go.

2

Occasionally, I think
he must dream of me
in a city far away
curving his full and sentimental lips
into his beard.

O Cretan lying
in blue basalt: three
thousand layers: your kids
and nannies bleat in herds
of calcined curls and twists.

And I'll not dare
this strong-lipped sea: I
rockjump pool to pool, island
to coastline
where the rock sticks.

I vote for nothing
on the coast, but sea
and tea bag tea; where
little men with bellies dance
to metal melodies.

3
– On the green sheets your
sinewy arms,
reed flutes, played me down
where wind flew
at the sea like a cat

all afternoon behind
sea-hit shutters:
my name cried like a
forgotten spell: and he
likewise crying before.

In the sea's thirst
indifferent and lavish, on
the rocks, where the teenagers
dive and sun – the sea
like an old worker

swilling and spitting,
hawking the rock out,
cleaning its salt mouth out
roughly: the same yesterday
as tomorrow – there

(against that black ring
that scratched round full

towns last night its
government's reeking fire,
its closure —)

there, in your two
disunited ways
as if calling on caves
of witches, come bait
and drum me with

your wishes, both of you
crying out hoarsely
for the underwater clasp,
her frogskin tuned and turned
to golden sea.

Your sailors' voices
in low tones
along the coast
where water works its farm
and the oblivious children sun.

The separation

'Why can't you live together'
the boy asks. He bends
away from the woman.
His profile is rigid, tired.
It's so late at night and
all evening they've quarrelled
and sworn, flung blue
murder of threats,
useless. And
when she asks for
his real worries, not homework,
not school, not friends, he
in quiet asks.
She knows he knows her reply,
steely and more helpless than when
long ago he asked 'why
can't I?' and got
answered 'because you
can't.' 'Because we can't'
finally and finally she answers.

Leaves

Leaves at this time
turn to red and gold and pale
washed off and down

skins of leaves from trunks
shed, are flayed, float
leave the ploughing bark

his hands take hers
hold hers to the sky –
rain and light stick back the thin forms –

and raise up the hands
dropping and whirling, rising and prancing
white, exhausted; the wind
silently lays them back.

The hawthorn

No   it's too much   this hand to
mouth
                    but   listen my
darling, what choice have we?

Cooped up like two kids by
the witch
                ah   but no witch
nor giant spelled such gratings

Two thickened magpies branch
and flop
                  through tanglewoods
we see in the pane

Go away to America   go I
shall live
                like a sow in
silk   when I live alone here

watching those thickhead magpies
wade
                through the black
stricken wooden hawthorn

Dear   what is your
countree

hold hands   when

Are there ever leaves?   Listen
outside
                        the glass
                        put your ear

not   not
overnight   ever?

Look up, look out

Anger
cool, calm and collected!
Not saying you bastard
but thinking it.

Look up, the New York statue
under her lightening points and
her outstruck arm holding the famed
fire: under her

heavy eyebrows she —
but only in the stone points of the
motionless eyes above the immigrants,
the pleaders of cases

or causes of liberty or right
coming in —
shows that kind of composed and
balancing dislike;

which she personally is prepared
to put up with, and be
used for Athena or Justice
or Liberty or America or whatever.

Io the wanderer

I   sound of myself

O   O   the baby's two eyes over the cliff's edge
                              what have we here?
O...O...O   the helterskelter smotherfaced giggle in
answer to the big gruff What Have We Here?

O   say our mouths
                          our red tissues amazed
confident   crying our due   our
dutiful sound
Words are hard
                      clicking of rows of hard wooden words
In feeble will   in delicious silence
our red lips cried out, a child,
and look!   she's laced in magic beads
                      she beams in amulets.

Vanity, smiles, fright in the
          moon's O
                          tissues scared white
                          (to a cow's white)

                              The increasing
salt cleft, the entranced and
      beguiled vault
                          the moon's word
                          (what have I here?)
Her bearing of the sun

Again and again daily and by century he
overbears her
that orange woodpecker terror
who pokes in and leans out on her

swaying elbow crook, her alder branch
He skis wide out in deep space
　　　　blue　green　black　burning　stippled
and striped cuckoo of the docile moon; and he
stings　jostles　taps the rump of the small
sparrow legged cow, till she flies
　　　　　　puffa puff, round and round　round
galloping her stretches – she clops out
the thousands year rule of great man.

Far from being her baby
　　　　　　　he's rapidly a city, a field
　　　　　　　of teeth, from each one
jump　　　　　　resplendent, fully armed missiles
and from each, a hundred warheads glitter.

So she flies through Europe, America, Asia and
at last in Egypt long before now, there so we
hear in peace from her tearing round, settled, lay
down on mud flats split by the sun's beak.

　　　　Golden flies are beaming
　　　　beneath a strobe light turning
　　　　round and round, puffa puff.

There reads a small old sign:
　　　Crane Birds and Pygmies Fight Here
There reads a big glitterbugging sign:

FILL UP HERE LAST STOP TO VEGAS

Too late　too late

　　　　The lunatic boy consults
　　　　the glasseyed mollusc
　　　　the lion lies down
　　　　on his four gold paws

Hermit by the well's lip, by the lorries of diamonds
and topaz turning, she squeezes in, fits in, begins to
speak:

of plump figs, strawberries and of
other hopeless fruit, of (with tears)
                            her stunted girl
blind, rag round her fly-bit eyes
misted, the flies that home in her feet
and build a nest, lay their rich ripe white
stacks of prodigal and organised eggs
My daughter is a blind cripple
Demeter
                a girl aged
         O   her mouth says   O

         Io   Io   Io
the I and O formula
of the sun and the purple mollusc   of men
of armies   I   and my big mouth
those openwide red lips in delicious
silence   in fear

                What have I here
The lion lies down on her four paws
flickering by the wooden well's lip
the hermit carves her abacus   the boy's
lost perhaps forever   the old gold fly
                    insists, we must be going on.

Dark

Everything's dark in the morning.
Just outside a phoenix
                    begins to call
at quarter to six.

At blue before dawn
(coming over the bulk of the roofs)
it whistles like a child
lazily from the hawthorn.

It's bunked outside
                    all night while
I have dreamt pain and all these
tears I can't get rid of.
Bird I can't see –
                    hear – can't see

Too far away

You are too far away
for my liking, my darling.

Three thousand miles of grey sea,
a watery chastity belt between us!

I want to cry but the tears don't
match that, the gulf

you opened, and locked
shut between us

the sea corset,
the huge shining belt.

The river, the child

And you   a chimera

a dozen horns   risky and impenetrable
in smoky bushes pearled with rain showers,
absurd too, in a boy's bunkbed
your feet stretching large cold and slender
over the edge

I fear and find
the chalk blue   dove grey
priest mask

my mouth I know is full of images
graven   chased
with bulls and monsters

but recently   I did dream
            of this birth:

            unlike your river
so green, swollen, punishing, roaring
swift, its icefloes carrying hippies
instruments flowers
and others carrying corpses, splayed
white on white
off white on white
livid on white   glass coffined
on the waters of turbulent downpouring.

Wax further smoothed by fur
            I had one child

he was born black and bullet headed:
his face and body slipped and slopped ivory
so easy   but then the head between
my legs   the waist garotted by bone

arse and spindle legs turn inside . . .
A voice says lightly   *push   bear down*
his shoulders broad, damp and ivory
we obeyed and he slid from my cunt.
I shit him with strong ease   he stops between me
Blank almond eyes eye back to me   the
black fringe over your brow.

Infant wreath   wreathèd   wraith child

     I woke up but the child
stays around   his eyes still into mine
he flexing ivory and bone and weight
(and softest   soft ear lobes   not to forget)

The loving red hen & the strong young fox

They're getting on fine
she's on her beam
he's crouching on the barn floor
she nods down, he springs up
For each a fine red feather
                  a handsome red hair
each doodling in its comfortable place
            each in its air or earth
but each to the other   up   down
           swing high
                     swing low

Then despair crows up in him
He fixes on her more blatantly, aims
bang! melts her, she wants whatever
              a feather for a red red hair

So she loses her balance
Mama!   falls into the sack
It's a stone floor after all

He never meant that
tells her off for letting him
stare her down like that
She knows it; only
sometimes her beak
gapes shrilly at his slant eyes
– she starts to sneer   oh your
floating autumn hide   oh your
       flashing titian hide   oh
yes maple leaved hair   oh

your ruff that embraces deep woods of snow
but I've no home to go now
but I can dance no more now
since you have broken my spring

He only meant, for his part
to eat in delicacy
to lick, to nibble
                Joy, hallowed
of the fox who munches up, the hen
        who's gone in . . .

and comes back later little by little, bit by bit?

She knows all that, she shared
the fever whining and snapping and shivering
between them in the air
                                between earth and beam

But now he has to starve.
Now there's only a stone in the sack
a broken hen statue
heroic embodiment of hen

a small chipped beauty   sad   sad

A feather floating out
                        for a red red hair

Note: In the traditional story, the Sly Young Fox traps the Little
Red Hen into falling off her beam into his waiting sack . . . Later she
escapes, replacing herself by a pile of stones . . .

Gilbert's Motel

My long hair is flickering
in the rain storm
and the sky increases from black
to an entire devoted grey.

The brown pelicans
have inserted their
boat-like bodies, their broadswords
into the swamps

and equally the humans
here, into their boxes,
their bare lime bedrooms,
their big brown old-fashioned TVs.

I watch the creek, belted flat
mist out of green waves.
Over the bridge the trucks
hurdle and slap right on.

Key Largo, 1983

Flipper at Key West

I saw four grey dolphins,
the first poked a football,
two clapped their flippers,
three jumped a pole,
the fourth, on antibiotics, wouldn't.

Really we had our mouths
open waiting for that
voluntary hurtling from here to
there, weight flicked up:
hooked on the red ball like them.

Forget the hop over the pole —
Solid ten foot muscled
dolphins entering a
slow triple leap, while
the fourth imitated weakly.

They don't escape, said our
loving yellow-haired guide, they
like our dead fish too much.
Even a tinsy bit afraid of the
live snappers that teem here.

Now see Duffy 'targetting'
as we say, on Tracy's hand
— give Duffy a well earned round.
We do, heartily. Remembering
'the upthrust of a dolphin

is like a nuclear missile'
admired the television man.
America salutes dolphins.
Out of the Base, US
defense against 'drugs and

communism' next door,
strides the new general:
the Navy calls on dolphins,
who still lead in sonics,
to train as underwater spies.

Outcry. Duffy in the pen
clicks amiably on.
Tracy feeds fish in 'slidable'
chunks to the dolphins'
beige tongues. And they

rove round the pool
after the show, surface,
heave back, twinkle an eye
sideways to inspect us
and glide down again, no interest.

Key West dawn

At once the dogs bark to each other;
but no wandering roosters, buried
by boulevards and carports.
The catbird mews in the pine feathers.

Last evening I drank myself
merrily with pink Seabreezes
into a night of the shivering horrors.
At the end: je ne regrette rien.

Like an old lady's gold dress
the dawn embroiders the curtain.

Watching American TV

I kept turning back to the preacher.
She was still at the mike
an hour later. I liked her
tip-tilted nose, her ambiguous glossy
black hair, I liked the
dove to eagle of her husky
voice, the breathy
listing of endless severe complaints
when she was sixteen, which afforded
her severe pains in the foot, ribs and
chest area, till faith healing to
her amazement 'Ah never would've
b'lieved' made it all possible, to
stand before the mike in crippling
heels for an hour shouting
hosannas from great lungs
at a TV crowd of
millions, including yours truly
amazed.

Vieux Carré

The first room was sunny with
flounces, overlooked a stranger's pool blue
green with banana plants. Steps
climbed to a dozen galleries.
I couldn't hop, skip our green

stairs. You called me Blanche Dubois
in the second room, inside
coral flounces and claret red plank
walls where we guessed slaves
had once lived. I wept,

argued, admitted your pointed
hard-loving tongue. In a salon
a butch boy entwined with
his small python, showed it off,
its head roved and flickered, a baby doll.

I walked out by the corner
bar, even at dawn smoky and
pounding inside; the odd van
or man down Dumaine, leaning by:
'Come with me? Anything you like

laid on.' I shrug him off, yawn
– what a night, hour after
hour of men zagged heel to
head like a black brown white
python twined on my flounces –

I delicately lick my dried lips –

Young men up in the birdcage
galleries, always with thin hips
and sandy moustaches, embrace
passionately. Light cooling it,
amber as skin through upstairs leaves.

New Orleans, 1983

What idiots lovers are

You meet a man
as tall as a redwood,
as sly as a garrulous blue jay,
as patient as a riding-horse.
You're scalding, your love's boiling
over – it surely is but
only sometimes. He's the same,
boiling –
same cauldron of
frangipani blossoms and toads
– The distance between the
two idiots narrows
to Achilles' tortoise. What
a puffing. And
then it stops – they
look down between their
toes, mingled – and each stands
wobbling on opposite sides.
What immense landscapes, canyons,
chasms, torrents pour between
these ten and ten toes.
Too great – the vertigo
is insufferable, the lovers cling, lean,
clasp like a church steeple, harder
and harder the cement, the
tongue and groove, the pebble and dash
– the vane cock dances in every
possible quarter, reconciliations,
rebirths. The pit underneath splits
the great tower
in the end, how can it not?
                              Helter skelter
you see the redwood heave and totter
the smashed jay feathers, the
horse hoof over ear,
the lot curl so slowly down

as if air could hold fancies
and their lovers up forever,
ball-eyed, clamped, grooved.
Pit-props – that's what
they make. Idiots of lovers
trying out edifices.

San Francisco, 1983

The woman alone

Deserted and not visited
by women, her own mother old,
here is a sad picture.
Why am I excluded? (She asks.)
Why the bread knife
           prickling against my finger?
The sharp meat knife
all through
has earned me such
exclusion. They're
not there, the busy bees,
the chatterers.
Men! That's it,
(she thinks over and over) they're
jealous, but why? They
have their well fleshed homes,
their cows and acres . . .

The nurse-shark-toothed
           following sirens
(she sang to weakly, hour in, hour out)
              insanely:
they'll not let me get away,
they're closed ranks, and the famous
golden hair has branched
to a laquered fence, the mirrors
coagulate when I look:
they round to bullets.

(She has the idea of being followed
inserted, like a tooth or a comb
              into the wrong head.)

Was it a lie (she wonders)
or a magic wish, the

woman who loved a woman?
No, she has met them.

Is it me? (She asks,
asking herself as if to a judge
– but who else is there?)
She's aware of her own
lacquered stockade – her
own palace of doped sleep.
             The push up
her garden path is in
all justice, not (she still
thinks) not so thorny,
not so hard won. Then,
             the palace:

(here her heart turns to lead)
the place itself is wrong,
sparse, an illusion, no
carpets and nothing in the
kitchen? (Her heart keeps melting,
the lead tears squeeze out.)

             The dwelling
(she must not cry like this:
her mother is too old)
is good. It will
be visited in due course.
(She was going to run away.)
The house is sound, reasonably
                stocked
no incandescent waking palace
but sound. (She
wanted to run away.)

She lights a fire
on stones blackened
by years of use:
to know where
to come back to.

She walks into the wood
with red hood
and basket, and bow
and silver-thonged
ankles: O huntress of women!
(My mother lies in there, living still.)

A Poem For Guatemala (1988)

A Poem For Guatemala

I hear this of Guatemala.
The Indians are driven like animals
far into the mountains.
Their villages are empty, their cornfields high with weeds.
The Indians are gunned into the wilderness.
The wild forest makes a burial of their homes.
Why is this land, soaring with purple mountains,
quartered by the helicopters, like terrible fever insects?
Their skulls, their bellies stream tongues.
They quiver lower with a thick pulse.
They're looking for morsels of the lost people.
Machine guns rake the tall pines, the little berry bushes.
I heard this of Guatemala.

Why does the Army rape
and hack with machetes the Indian women?
The morning star has lost the dawn.
Why does the Army behead the children? Sinking of light.
Who is the Army that more malignant than the fever insect
bites a village to death
and its worm guzzles the carrion? The young soldiers
shoot into the corpses. They are shouting and laughing.
On the sidewalk outside the grocery store, on the steps to the
Church, in the dark adobe houses and in the
beggars' torn down canopies, the bodies lie in piles.
'Your bodies are the temple of the bleeding Christ'
says the young priest. He gives up his own.
The Archbishop dines with the General.
I heard this of Guatemala.

This is the wound in the side. No prayer
to the Mother, the Earth, has stopped the flow.
The taking of the children . . .
the stealing of the children . . .

Many soldiers are the sons of Indian dead. Their mothers
and fathers were martyrs. The Army killed them
slowly over fires. They cut off the parts of their bodies.
A soldier guarded the bodies for many days from
burial, until the wild beasts were finished eating.

The Soldier

And this is the open wound. No prayer in secret
sent to the Mother, the Earth, has stopped this further flow,
this second weakening of the Indian body.
Many a soldier is the son of Indians.
The Army took away the child to an orphans' home.
They taught him loyalty to hatred of his parents.
Many a soldier is the son of Indian dead.
He is sent to fight in other areas
against other villages unknown to him.
There are falls of blood in the mountains
to the gun of the soldier.
As a boy his elders taught him to pray first
to what he must of his need kill.
They taught him to know his own spirit animal, his *nahual*.
What is the nahual of the soldier?

The Model Village

If afterwards the soldier comes to his own
village, he must join the 'civil patrol.'
And the patrol guards the new village now
which is a pen for the slow blundering obstinate
work mules who must be barred up at night otherwise
they would kick up their heels and escape into the forest.
This is the model village, which is a model pen.
All night in the model pen the starlight searches
and the four winds have each a wooden tower.
The pen is located next to the half-built motorway.
All day the weak stagger under earth loads
and they drag the concrete beams.
They drop, they burn out.

The Finca Owner

Up inside the forest the old houses burned easily,
palm wall and palm thatch. Nothing much is left,
except the land unharvested. On stones
Indian blood has woven at gunpoint its traditional pattern.
New harvesters come, machines, sheds, roads for lorries.
The land becomes a proper business, the finca owner
    measures
his land as his tailor measures his belly. It is said
God makes the Indians from maize; the owner is now
the man of maize, he is the woman of maize, he is the child
of rack and ruin, he is the coffee ghost, the cotton ghost,
the sugar ghost, he is the steer on the loose,
the mechanical horns have no prayer in their ploughing,
the land he swallows yields its fruits,
he spits out what yields no profit
such as dreams, grinding stones, the speaking in other
    tongues
of cooking fires, gods of no name he knows, the ash
of the disappeared. He has no skill but blood weaving.
Down here the people weave a village of memory
inside the steel thorn thicket of the pen.

The Officer

The soldiers once came to the village of memory.
The ladino officer laughing once human being instructs his
    men
to rape, burn, flay, crush, shoot, apply simple electrodes.
Brutes, he jokes. Meaning all parties.

The villager is pressed into the civil patrol.
The ladino officer laughing once human being orders
the man to set alight to his good neighbour.
From the mouth of laughter the tusks are hung with flesh.
The officer jokes:
Are these rituals simple enough for you? To scream and
    sweat,

to fall down dead. I'm ordered to inform you,
you have been allocated to these duties, either or both.
Collectively you shall die in spirit, singly die in the flesh
and in hundreds of thousands you shall do this
for you are the most numerous in this land
and your voice goes back into the quiets of time.
You grow tired.
– Come with us, you shall be unburdened of your life's most
burdensome load, by courtesy of the Army and
the Land Businessman – and these two
make a one continuous killing.

Duty

'I am doing my duty' says the nervous soldier 'we are
hunting the subversives.' 'Who are the subversives?'
He laughs. He hoists his rifle. The Indians,
an old woman, a man, three children lie in the bracken
waiting for the squad to pass by.
'Hey you, where are your papers?'
I hear this of Guatemala.

The Clinic

The woman goes to a clinic to give birth. A poor ladino
woman. The place is clean. There are hot water and
medicines. But first she must sign the doctor's paper.
Her cross. She returns home after the birth. Where is
the baby, your black-haired, brown skinned baby? The
sling on your back is empty. My arms are empty. My womb
is empty as a gourd. They scoured it like the clothes on
a washboard. It wrinkles as small as a finished gourd.
As for the baby, they told me it died at birth. So I
never saw its sleek hair like a feather of night. My milk
didn't touch its suckling mouth. My forefinger didn't
lift its wandering fist. Its mouth lies dry and I am a
dried gourd until my own time.

You were told a lie. We heard they killed your healthy
baby, in secret – they threw away the body.

Thus, doubly, the poor die. Indians. Ladinos. Old. Young.
I hear this too of Guatemala.

The Morning Star

When will this land be free?
And the villages be uncovered from the tractor tread and
the flattened ranges of the loosened bull?
When will the Indians sow their seed corn
and the children grow tall in their parents' houses?
When will the jungle, dangerous with wild beasts, be more
dangerous than the city of General the wild boar?
And his dens are roofed and slick with
the half seen web of the spider coming down
coming down for its dollar piece.
When will the morning star rise and dawn come
and the land be free?

When the General ceases to crucify those he calls
animals, Los Indios.
Then the wild boar will lie down with the Indian child.
When the foreign investor requires a just wage
for his contracted workers, young, old, Indian, ladino, all.
Then the preying spider will contract its web.
Which is made in America and therefore not so hard to see.

The Straw Men Begin To Speak

When will the land be free?
When the Powers of the world are pushed by their people
like ants tugging and pushing at stiff straw men
and they stand themselves up and say to America:

Where is the land of the free? For sure not in your
backyard which we have quite agreed is your backyard.
We have heard the sticks of your agents laid on

the backs of your yard boys.
And we did not hear their thwack as they descended.
We heard the groans in the slums and on the
assembly lines and between the piles of the
excellent restorative coffee bean that
is loaded into ships for your people and for ours.
And we did not hear the groans –
any that heard we called ignorant, evil –
But the cries of the dead are too shrill:
they reverberate across the oceans.
We blocked our ears but we are surprised;
for such faint faraway cries they get louder.
These spirit cries are beginning to come to our notice.
Reluctantly we must bring them to yours.
For when America
our shining knight, our platoon leader
shouts out 'Freedom,' we hear also an
echo of voices that also cry for Freedom.
To want Freedom from Freedom!
This paradox is beginning to itch a corner
of our brains.

The Dream

And at last the smooth eyelids of America open from
their doze in a spray of perfume in a parlour in a web
of shining strands that stretch sea to sea and
way beyond up to the stars, a white house shining
all crease free. And out of fur stretches the spider
languorously. And it rears up on birthday cake candle packets
of pointed missiles. And softly America answers:
I have dreamt I ruled a prison yard of slaves and
the reason was to make bananas a few cents
cheaper in Miami and in Dallas and in
my great cities of the East Coast and of the
North and of the Midwest and of the West Coast.
And the dream was true. And I will stop entertaining myself
with my box of fireworks and my puppet show.
And instead I will back freedom as I promised to do.

And after the true dream of America the land of Guatemala
will be rid of the white house strands that shore up
the den where the wild boar snarls. The people will
pour out from behind barbed wire, walking home under
the morning star.

I dreamt this of Guatemala
from the hope of peaceful people.
After which I heard these hopeful sounds of freedom
such as drawled snarls, drawing-room sniggers, bar farts
and fatassed cackles: Keep dreaming, cretinos
keep weaving those bright dream patterns, keep hoping!

The Dream Patterns

Once everywhere
the dream patterns sang in the branches,
clouds and sunlight moved in broad train
over the lands of the Mayans
who are the oldest of the peoples of Guatemala
and the Mayans have uttered such patterns, elder to child,
over four hundred years of auto da fé
that to this day they sound among
the fluting of airy waters, among the hills.
And they sound in the aqueous sighing
of the emerald vassal of the feather lords of the Maya:
which is the quetzal bird whose plumes the lords stole
but they would set the bird free
to redress its gorgeousness . . .
But nowadays 'quetzal' is cash,
a bird stamped on coins pocketed, modern money pattern.
Being chased to vanishing, adopted then
as the country's emblem of freedom, the metal creature
old cynic, sighs on the face of capital
'Freedom here anyway.'
The living quetzal, they say,
in prison breaks its heart and dies . . .
So, in the compound, the dreams are kept
like the Host on the tongue

like an inner lock on the mind
as a warning of gods
against the breaking of the heart.
After four hundred years there are the patterns.

Maya, moon and sun shine like candles in your eyes.
Like fruit and tinsel and shells and mirrors and bells.

How indefatigable you are with the plant sowed,
weeded, watered and slowly greening.

How you feast the child and the growing one
and the harvest and the cloud passing
inevitably over the mountain. With tinsel and shells
and mirrors and fruit and bells and incense and praying.

Through the middle of the dark jungle
you hoist a flare of pine resin.
Moon, sun and clear star are your lighted resin.
Through thorny gullies, single file by precipices
you set your faces towards the green planting.
With tinsel and mirrors and fruit and gourds and singing.

Maya, moon and sun shine like candles in your eyes.

Cabracán

And I heard this, of the earthquake
once called Cabracán by the Quiché Maya.
How earthquake or Cabracán threw up the fields and houses
and people, and during this last decade one threw up
    another:
a Cabracán of many voices
restless . . . erupting that the children must have food
to live past the age of five. And the wild boars
laughed, and launched farts for tear gas.
And the land was dug with the tusks of civil war.
Mines boobytrap the trail. They cut the walker in pieces.
The country is cut in pieces.

The people become subversives, for this is what
their Government calls them. But they are the rebels.

The Armed Rebellion

The young people go up into the rain forests.
They have nothing but a pack of tortillas,
sticks, machete, stones, a hoe. They are ladino, Maya.
They are the guerillas. Now the guerillas have nothing but
tortillas and rifles, grenades and mortars.
The soldiers have rifles, mortars, rocket launchers, tanks,
fighter planes, gunships. They asked their foreign advisers
how they fought the gooks in Vietnam.
The guerillas are skinny and ragged. They sleep in
the tusks of night.
The soldiers are taller. They are given some meat.
The jeeps return to barracks at nightfall. The soldiers
are paid little.
The guerillas have no pay. Anger pays them.

They have set up anger in the emplacement of the hills.
The metal of their anger
being the heat of the General's greed and the
coldness of the corruption of the General's men.
This anger smokes like a burning palace,
it smokes like an expensive restaurant, like a skyscraper
wreathed in its scarlet laurel COCA COLA.
And the shells of the guns of the anger are
packed in hard with the hate
of the cotton pickers whose twelve-year-old son
was wrapped in a cloud of insecticide as he picked
the hard cotton fluff, and he died.
And the shells of the anger are cased in steel
vows, the vows sworn over the ditch where the shantytown
leader floats face down in the grey before dawn
and the range of the anger is like the
mountains themselves, blue and visionary. But the guns have
    talked

daily to the grunting pig in its den; they have learned
the small-eyed aim of its charge and
themselves learn to charge in blood.
But she who ignites the charge is the oldest of all,
the crone, the raker of the city dump.

The Dump

Where on this bright morning the grandmother rakes for
the leavings of the banquet last night. There was a
feast given in honour of the Ambassador: fish, quail,
  chickens
suckling pigs, veal and several tints of years of wines. From
California flew on ice plump and well manured strawberries.
From Washington the Ambassador. A charming display to
  end:
of the traditional costumes of our adored country.
And the well mannered Ambassador is instructed and
  charmed and
expresses this to our new President, to which the General
lights his cigar.
And today the grandmother rakes back the chicken leg
that the Ambassador forgot to finish as he watched with
crinkling eyes the costume of her tribe. She plucks it
hungrily out of the sweet rot under the sweet
blue sky. Dipped in cigar ash, casseroled in filth, the
chicken bit comes into her skin and bones hand. Dry-eyed,
her stare turns on the city.

The City, Xabalba

Anger of the just. Slow burn of a peaceful people. Anger.
The right to sow and reap a piece of earth. For their
bleeding Christ thousands have made a temple. Temple upon
temple upon temple. A reasonable even a small demand.
Timidly the Archbishop pleads with the General. Candy and
Pepsi-Cola and cotton T-shirts. The workforce is docile
and learns fast, say the T-shirts.
I heard this of Guatemala.

Lately, this too of Guatemala.
Chanting – marching – scattering under the farting gas –
reforming – like mercury drops – rolling together –
different, centripetal chemistry at work in the city.

And a widow, forty-five seeming eighty or a hundred and
     five
so lean with work and with murderous events, walks
four hours to the marble-denned city. Squats by the doors
all day. Where is Pascuale, where is Maria? I have not
seen him for two years, for two months, for two
weeks I have not seen her. I saw his body, she was
lying by the road. I don't speak the language:
but the bravest women fly like birds, messengers
out to the universe. They tell the universe
how like birds we are trapped and shot down
by the lords of Xabalba, which is the under region,
how we sit in the House of Punishment
which is crammed with the poor,
how wild beasts measure out our fields for money,
how we fall like feathers off bones of the emerald bird.

Banish the cruel men. You are our President.
Say the moon and sun of her eyes.

Banish all cruel men. Say her eyes.
Watchful strangers in the strange region.

The one who is not for me is against me,
I will sit till with my hands I open
the marble jaws of Xabalba, the den, dark Purgatory.

Till I see the dawn like a deer run all over the mountains
and we are led from moon to sun by the morning star
each night to the day

and the children of Guatemala grow again
like yellow corn or stone towers or green trees
and my bowed eyes pierce up to the heart of Heaven.

Hear me.

Storm at the end of a Greek summer

The withering geraniums,
under one red clothes peg
on the line,
stiffen and snake up to the lightning.

One clothes peg and nothing
on it, sharp scarlet; we
brought in the clothes and the –
olios, olios, shouted the stormwarner.

I walk to the harbour
under sentence of lightning.
Ships, boats tremble there,
water pinned flat

by dot on dot of rain,
by its blue grey surges
pulsing across – catching
me – I run back in the gusts.

Over our aged olive tree,
our cobbled roof,
sort of ours for four weeks . . .
the sky booms, overhead

and far off softly:
in a cyclone's ring, round
the silver ravines around Lakka.
Then, finally, this

crustacean, thickened grey sky,
opens its wings.
The sun is bare, before dusk,
sharp gold, you'd think motionless.

Note: olios means 'all'.

My mother's house

Doves, crying to each other
raucous and moody –
doves flash past the
windows, yearning –

circle the topmost pines.
One, trapped in the
green fir tunnel by
the tennis court

pants and crashes on
the netting, its fan
tail quilled a stiff oyster
shell rosy grey

till it ricochets
out, and flees on through
a sunbeam I saw
in a child's book

of the Holy Land.
A German Christ child
bouncing with gold hair
across a field of roses

daisies and cornflowers
to the Garden of Evening:
black shadows and doves
white on a crude cypress.

Note from *The Book of Changes*

Clinging is fire, the sun, the middle daughter.
It means coats of mail and helmets.
It means lances and weapons.
What does the armourer say? The riddling
of the lance, bending, crushing,
smoothing out to gleaming. A ring of hammers,
their drip and spark out and down.
Among men it means the big bellied.

It is the sign of dryness. They say it is
the tortoise, the crab, the mussel, the hawkbill tortoise.
Belly slow, beak moving prudently among dry
grasses, this way and that.
Imagine the snail and its sister the crab from
the thin ebb, wandering on the floor by
the armourer's dirty foot. How would
they find their way out? How to avoid
the dark fire? the hammer blow? They crawl
into a belly of ashes. Meanwhile the maker
of helmets clings to the dead article he knows
because of its beauty.
The black blue case of a mussel is
trivial, the wrapping box of a delicacy. But I worship
its motionless changing colours.
They say among trees
it means those which dry out in the upper
part of the trunk.
Thick headed. Small brains. Hair pulled round nothing.
Dry, the middle daughter knows the
sputter of the unmaking fire: its grunting timber yard,
its beach of calcined shells and houses of lower forms.
She knows the rocketeer's ambition
he concentrates in a lance momentarily
incandescent.

Madame Boucher by Boucher

— the Frick collection, New York

Madame Boucher has
black eyebrows, a tight waist,
pink satin slippers. Silks,
ribbons, bags all over the floor.

Monsieur Boucher set up
this *déshabillé* with hand
akimbo satisfaction. The mending
on the stool, the tassels
twining from the drawer.
A la mode a little robed
ample stomached Chinaman
squats on the wall cabinet
over the pink chaise-longue.
His rose and white skinned
apple of a household slut.
She compresses her mouth shut.
And half smiles when Boucher
looks up; her brows are black,
her large hand rests her head.
She is thinking of noons,
of rides in the Tuileries and of
less careful eyes; also
of her subtle soup the maid
is simmering dry while
she's set simpering
on the chaise-longue; or simply
of lobbing the affable Buddha
through the long tulle-robed
windows that look on the Tuileries.
Tu es dans la lune, he smiles.
Her great jet eyes slide
away and she half smiles.

She'll make his soup –
her lovers, maybe. Their bliss,
her beauty and his genius,
chez Boucher that's the picture.

Sciatica in Esher in 1984

Even the Scargill foamers
   are speechless suddenly
over their potty azaleas – flower
   of the luxurious South East
or of acid Scottish hotels.

They are carried screaming
   like wets or wimps on
boards to bed for six weeks.

They look pale and stern as
   the Great War, as they go in
to be skewered and fused.

They can't blame the miners
   for slipped discs and stuffed
bellies over the azaleas, though
   they would like to.

For example Owen

A question to four deaths:
Wilfred Owen, France 1918
Ernst Tauber, France 1918
David Tinker, off the Falklands 1982
Armando Souda, off the Falklands 1982

An officer, a good shepherd
who thought he should go
with his doomed flock, with love.
He asked, how could he sit in comfort
even in conscience and inside prison
while his men passed in their thousands
under the hand of the giant into the cave.
So he went back in there. He 'went west'.
A bullet smashed him on a canal bank
a week before Armistice.
The very bridge (over the Sambre)
was never built that his men
tried to build. Almost all of them
were 'casualties'. He was 'struck'
while 'calmly' helping to fix the
duckboards into place. There,
Owen handed himself into the war.
He 'fell' among planks awash,
hit and hit, smashed, gouged into
springing arrowhead shards under
the fire; by virtue of a crafty
self-deceit, by reason of a huge desire
for a virtuous reason to live, out of purest
nobility; among debris slithering
across Lethe, planks drifting waterlogged
and sideways, batted by each other,
nudged by shapes hunched underwater
like giants; he fell down among
matchsticks carrying the random and
slumped dead making a crossing.

Planks for white crosses
like plague signs stuck up forever
and tended, as if the crushing plague
might lift, one day, from our houses
if the signs are kept fresh
and we remember.

We don't forget.
The lethal courage of the lamb.
Our bloodgeld two wars long.

From old colonial days
a malaria flickers underskin
a muttering sootfall
of sorrow and love, hate and revenge
upworded to the old noble
pro patria decorum est . . . Gasbag
speeches unworded to the pure brass blare
of Downing Street. Upcoding into
computers, signals, radar, rockets, missiles
and three torpedoes
to hit, hit, hit
'a likely violation of the exclusion zone'.

By Sambre
they hadn't invented bodybags
with plastic zips. Stretchers they had.

"All a poet can do today is warn."
With what caught pride does the young
officer draw up to his peaked cap.
In the photograph
Owen smiles with his expressive
eyes and his plump cheeks. In the next,
a glad, rangy face, fair hair,
David Tinker, Lieut. RN, on board, ploughing
the South Atlantic, at first ardent,
then writing home, "the professional forces
of both sides" – he was one –

"do what they are told. If two
megalomaniac idiots tell them
to beat each other's brains out they do."
A week later an Exocet
'beat its way' to his cruiser.
Among those burned to death was Tinker.
'To the end he was calm and brave.'
Tinker, David . . . soldier, sailor. Souda, Armando.
Tauber, Ernst. Owen, Wilfred. Smiles. Rictus.
Caught in smiles, some. Zipped up.
Flown home to a salute. Interred. Crossed white.
With what ritual pride does the young
officer draw up to his peaked cap.

"My subject is War and the pity
of war" . . . Owen
Tinker . . . Tauber . . . Souda.
O passionate lovers of the public virtue
O young wisemen of pity,
how is it, deftly, deftly, you kill
but yourselves only? The flatterers
salute you out.

You golden fleecy flock, why run
before the brokers and the farmers of blood?
They buy and sell in tender carcases
on war's slab, and in between
in peace – they speculate in futures.
While the young rams breed up
glittering with a hard urge to wrestle death.

The flatterers have released you
among the stumps of French woods or on
sheep islands among cavelike seas –
Here are the high-powered assault rifles,
the heat-sensing missiles entirely
under your hands –
Turn around, look round behind you.
See them sitting comfortably behind you

in their bunkers, on silk chairs.
There they work.
They sail corpses like paper boats.
Make another formation, brothers –
Lock your sights – Advance
on these rears – satiny rear ends.
Your words become your weapons, your weapons
are your words; licking across the ceremonial grounds:
breaking to the rear: No more!
                No more your burden beasts!
                Our missiles stuff your arses
          so no more death trumpeting and trumpeting.

So say it to your flatterers.

Turn, soldiers of unfreedom, look round.
We who love you, who are your own people
we offer a docile back-up
to those who farm your deaths –
Turn and curse us
out of our timidly ranked houses
from which we offer you up.

But you say: Orders are orders.
But you say: I cannot leave my men, my brothers.
But you say: Now this is my only life
             so has to be my death.
             No one at home can know our deep bonds.

I shout back through the dumb wood
across the bloody channels:

You are the soldiers, not them.
Envisage a life, not a death
in brotherhood – is that impossible to men?
This question is for you.
You are tied to a killing post by garlands
marvellous and phantom as poems.
Whip vines or gossamer, what garland ties

you to your killing post?
Which one, steel or breakable?
This question is for you.

Owen . . . Tauber . . . Tinker . . . Souda
it was the question I burned to ask
of the brave shepherds, the brave sheep, dead mutton.

A little medley for Civil Defence

Duck and Cover – United States CD slogan
Protect and Survive – British CD slogan

Ducks and survive
waddle to the gang plank
looking for grub in the bank.
Underground the steak smoulders,
the wine grows body, the Cadillac steams.
On top of living we survive
or subvive, or not we
but a few – d'you know them?

His little girl feeds Daddy

– TV preview of Budget Day in the eighties

Here's
a sight of the boar
head in closeup, mounted
stuffed on a wall, relaxed
before his tusking of
widows, disabled, geriatrics . . .
Freckledy
not Heath pink but teacup
rose and cream, roly fleshed,
prince never more, the
broad muzzle juts out:
today he's just Daddy Bearkins.
On the great knee sits
Goldilocks, plaited, clean-
eared, muslinned, she's
in no danger, she's no orphan.
The face
above works pink
lips to stretch sleepily
wide and to smile on his little
love. She turns her slender
shoulder, twists up and . . .
into her Daddy Bear's
maw, over short teeth,
across a lower lip
maintained replete on chins,
she passes a sugary bik;
the face
is almost too stuffed
to chew. Is thus
kept going, on extract of
millions of such small fry
– a consumer of such
prodigious hypnotic suction,
it could claim the victims

place themselves in
                        the gullet
of the face and close
the jaws behind them.

This lumbering face
            can charge

Note: the Chancellor was Nigel Lawson (since ennobled).

A harmless day at Greenham

A harmless day at Greenham.
One soldier behind the Orange gate
eyeing his toe, looking
as gloomy as a black pudding.

A cloud bank of that sagging grey
peculiar to English Novembers.
A barrelled fence of snarled erections
containing not much, a couple

of logo towers, a mound or two
of burial chambers. I've read
they call them silos, as if
they held wheat. Outside

the colour of a woman's long scarf –
a woollen rainbow. Mud. Cold.
A fire, with chipped planks and
furze. A kettle we must hide

from the Government. Twice
a day it steals pots and pans.

Flame tree   the Amazon expedition of the famous naturalist Louis Agassiz, 1862–63

Madame Agassiz
in her own right is an angel,
so says William James, expedition member.
She stands vivid but sweaty
propped and *soigné* in skirt upon skirt
– for Alexandrina is her speed.
She peels her blue eyes for some aerial petal
on which to float the senses
under the net these long river nights
noisy with whoops and whistles.
Natural hope, but there he is flat out
what with all day the natural world.

Her name has not much to do with tropic forests
or the leap of monkeys up tree trunks
beasts to which her mistress compares her:
Look, Alexandrina! Up. Up. There! Go fetch
the flowering branch.

. . . The servant's hair
is a great coiffeured Afro, a stately frame
to her rococo mouth and lucent barricaded gaze.
'. . . having,' writes Madame facing,
'in her extraordinary hair standing out
all round her head the mixture
of the two races, the Indian length
combined with the Negro crispness.'
Her use, apart from blossom brought down
to blotter, is to prepare skeletons
of fish caught in the Amazon
for Monsieur to christen, stick and stuff.
The account says nothing else.

Named for a library ticket out of old Egypt.
What was her family?
Name of a white conqueror of speed.
Dwindled to 'drina', to suit the 'monkey-like' girl
who 'intelligently' typed the bones.
The woman, her hardy skeleton
long gone through earth to transmutation
into the auras that rock by day
over the forests of Brazil —
she has rendered the passion flower and the trumpet vine,
the wood of life, flame of the wood, flame tree,
shower of orchids; she has named the river's force
into which under leaves: a tributary: one of millions:
her supplanted name has poured.

2

The hardwood tree grows tall
by grace of the clouds.
The vapour floats above the fountain trees,
result, cause, ascending, falling.
How the mists feint and fold away
secretly the moth, the toucan, the spider, the jaguar.
'I shall never cease,' wrote the young Agassiz
'to consecrate my whole energy
to the study of nature; its powerful
charms have taken . . . such possession
of me . . . I shall always sacrifice
everything to it.'

3

Monsieur Agassiz
has gone home to applause;
the decks of his steamers are waist high in flesh;
120 species, of which ⅔ are 'unknown'.
Who follows the sage of fish?
The naturalists of São Paulo, Rio, Miami and Houston
are out collecting. This will take time.
It is projected, with luck and capital

and labour and demand, in 35 years
Amazonia will be collected. In short
a crisp sacrifice in the making
for the great-great-grandchildren
of the woman of extraordinary hair.
They are as thin as gar and do not now
shin up trees in the country of monkeys.

The botanist sees the 100 foot tree.
The botanist saws the 100 foot tree.
Here is a new
                playground.
                            Here are
                                    the playboys.
        The tree becomes a
                            two by four.
                                        See.
                                            Saw.

Bauxite, manganese, petroleum, gold.
Come, disperse these mists!
Till nothing's there to support their witness.
Let the valuable geologist dig his garden.

Ash and Senhor Ass the consecrator
(Come, disperse these mists!)
prepare a skeleton.
Let the valuable geologist dig his garden.

Till nothing is there to support their witness.
Come, disperse these mists.

Finally: Ethiopia

people arriving in their thousands
many of them on the verge of death.

Heavy rain throughout today
but with bright intervals.

That's the news and weather
at ten past nine.

This week's composer Dvořák
took much of his inspiration

from Slavic folk melodies

plaintive rhythms, evoking
the sufferings of generations

yet also acceptance, with its
wistful, ultimately consoling resolution.

Swinging

Sonny Rollins
stood on Brooklyn Bridge
for four years
and blew and blew   figuring
this and that
after Bird died   and
                until
he was clear to walk forward again.

They say you could hear the sax
groaning and crying
above the percussions of the cars
and the barely pounding bass
      wind over the East River
      all day fisting
     across one thousand cables

Like a feather
      brushing sunlight
          on its own   until

it came for earth again

flew   like silver in a cool fever
          into Manhattan.

Which goddesses are YOU?

– book advertisement in
The Women's Review of Books

Not so damn easy to find
the strange one, that one
without gender or tissue
who must clench fists.

Easier to have fun with
Athena, Aphrodite
Hera; be wise Thursdays,
my thighs sticky wide

all weekend, and
on Mondays hang out
the washing, and the
straightforward Joves down

side up to cool off.
But for iron days and water days
like Wednesdays or the
unsexed passage of

time, where are the fists
of the strange one?
Curled like runts so
tight inside; not godlikely   .

to sculpt a drip drip
or smash these iron gutters of days.

All night long in Brooklyn

Cop cars squeal, howl and gasp
across the grid pattern. In my sleep
huge worms fight at intersections,
clapping and batting their brazen wings:
a Clang . . . Clang, sprouting inside
the two beat squeal. These
are the fire-engines come
swinging. Around this neck of
the brownstones and the big Navy
blocks we're a tiltyard all night
for dragons and marshals. They use
the breezy hours to boom and
yowl, yah! yah! over each crossing.
The sleepers, packed upstairs and stairs,
like steers, or peasants
are to be kept a shade edgy:
on their feet, shadow danced;
malleable, or anyway a shade
deferential, on sidewalks
glass crazed: wing
upon wing of dreamers.

Gulf shallows

– off Key West

I pulled taut an edgy sloe horizon
of rough cloud and full sea:
it banded like a runner's tape.
                    Today
the sun clarifies and clarifies, an agent;
brimfull and deceitful in fact.
The sea flares from the speedboat
for marathons, where cormorants
with muscular wings graph
the fields moving, neck and
belly to wave, executors
of my eye, runners who vanish.
Some place they leave, at or before the edge
where the jade and milky blue and
silvered and opal ranges wash through
the cordon and sky can't be sky,
where the edge had been, so I was clear.

My eyes idle. I can't impose or construct. . .
The blue fields I drafted have preceded.
I blank out into the escaping, where
am I heading

                        species   orders
    kingdoms

            sun deceiver   sea   lies

The hoop that barrelled the sun,
is it intact, unburst
by the fermentations, is there the
sloe blue circle, like a quoit
around us, underneath or behind
the white games of the sun?

I catch the hot red of my eyelid.
The colourless wink of a butterfly
scrapes and flickers: eyelashes
pause, whatever I see, across
my retinas like the veins of wings,
the legs of a new insect
uncramping and disentangling before it
delivers itself from gauze and fluid
and prances out of eyesight
into a flimsy dabble
                              a black drop
          a nearly transparent stopper of air

Love Lane, Key West

To go down Love Lane
you have to walk through the debris
first, which are rotting palm fronds, a pile,
and four lidless garbage cans, green and brown,
brimfull. The thin orange cat hangs
half in and the little black dog
drags a bag full of tins and Kentucky fries
sweet with ash and ants and the runny slide
of fast food out onto the parking lot
and goes to sleep and the sun gets stronger
and stronger.

        You and I walk down,
walk weightless or nearly so in the pool
underneath the small palms and the bougainvillea,
the nonstop red and purple and scarlet flowers.
My vagina is full of you and
you are laughing and so am I,
your hands pulling me back, your hands
your palms hold me by my breasts
gently easing me back onto you;
on the contrary your lips from above
the wide wet lips of a genial husky –
a merdog up from the beach . . .
over my cheekbones, over like a bunch of ripples,
over my plastered eyebrows, neat bones,
my hair rattails, mouth laughing, open wide
riding your human cock and your mouth
biting your swishing hands, under
the fronds, unable to stop laughing,
under the fence, under a tin lid of heat
vanished off me, drawn skyward
the constant pressure; that time no
coming down, no it was I going out
airily with you, in company with you, in

myself, I in water and freely within
and having scope, land and light strength
to move in all ways.

Anna the Italian

Like a little nodding mandarin
Anna, sun faced, brown buttered,
entices me to her cottage room
by a blue velvet pool.

She lies back, slender and floppy,
nothing to do all day
all summer in the ferocious heat;
her dark brown hair curls wet

against her boatwoman tan,
against her dark child's eyes.
She tells me of her 'tresora',
I dive, she says, and giggles.

Barracuda

Under a pall of crisp fruited
orange stemmed seaweed
hangs the sea tiger.
A white substantial flank.
My head's half turned in
its mask, scoping the green
halls of six foot water, nearly
empty halls stretching all ways
over dark rush beds,
odd convoys of pale snappers
in threes or fours, wandering
half visible. I was edging
to my right against the waves
to circle the weed mat
with its cloudy undershadow.
I was seawise in my simple
dislike. In and out of my eye's
jump I caught its long hull
striped, unstirring, silver, attentive.

It lies suspended on the shadowed
side of the pier, or by a rock
wasting time and my nerves
and doing nothing; like a
stuffed white and charcoal striped
pike someone caught and mounted
on the dark chimney breast high
over the mantel and under
the heavy vine of the moulding.
The mirror over the mantelpiece
runs without a word into a salt
hall of shifts and screens.
And out of the folds on to
a retina gawping and flickering
away as I curve for the light
clamps an eye, a lip, a jaw.

The obsession
slides under the sea clusters.

But the barracuda lying in
half dark under the shadow of
the weed is no one's mania:
a spurious mirror image
for our shifts and screens.
It rocks back and forth, idling,
smiling the bad conscience smile
which is a phoney . . . Except
for sure it scares what's larger,
white tentacled: me.
Smart that first pike
who pulled its dirty meaningful grin
and knew it was meaningful.
The plainer truth is, that recessed lip
supports a raft of teeth.
Do something stupid such as
tease the fish, or such as spear
another fish with this one around
and the scent flowing will launch
it right in without respect of bodies.
Let be however –
(and wear no metal in the water
like a silver pass of fish scales
in case of error –) Let be:
it won't flee, but invisibly
back off and surrender path, then
watch and hang again.

I flap past with ray-like calm.
A slight eyewhite tremor inside
the mask – a quick confession of sins
autonomic in a minute swerve.
Girl, that's it, I do not wound
nor do I offer the shine of a wound.
Not a stomach knot more
now that I know this
barracuda like a blood relation.

January in Margaret Street

An old Black woman

                              sits in a middling

                                   blue print dress

     sits rocking

Crickets tap tin spoons.

Two powered male basses

                   New Age humdinging

                                  the Sunday noon

         hereabouts not a soul

Lustral   air-stunners   party-givers.

Three Christmas palms

               fronting her yard

                       are bound in blue

      and in silver

On her nape her grey hair inclines to a bun.

Psalm of tinsel

             binding the trunks

               spiralling into the trunks

               of spiral streamers

Plumb   of tornado air.

Roof rats

Roof rats also nest in palms.
When the coconuts are ready,
to the annoyance of the owner
who has sat in his apartment below
with the TV and a crate of Milwaukee
all these months,
the rats drill into the shaggy heads
to suck the thin milk. Over the husks
they twine, sucking.
They spreadeagle their pink hands.

For other food or for the moonlight
they cruise below.
They hare over the downlands
of silver gables tiled in aluminium.
They jump down by disordered hair,
the wiry plaits and hanks of ficus branches,
bell pulls passing upper veranda
to lower veranda, home of a white turret
the boudoir of Mrs Carrasco;
or the crazy cottage next door,
its gate of hen wire,
its propped car – 'This car is not abandoned'
its plastic pelican, its Milwaukee man.

And so to the windy pavement
where the green coconuts blow down.

They bang, now and then, in the night.
They roll in among the seamed brown ones
piling the dry, blossom filled gutters.

And my son slept in the sitting-room
when he stayed with us

You lay under a creamy, baby soft blanket.
Your shoulders were, morning after morning,
cinnamon brown, loose, large and patched
red where the sun had broiled you out
cycling. Against our clinking and padding,
door latches, the toilet, coffee ticking, the
swish of the rowing machine on the deck
you dug into sleep. Your hair was salty
and wavy, punk cut, stiff with sea –
its glimmering coral and tangleweed long cut –

I cut across the other side to the bathroom
seriously quiet, a mother who tried
to leave your dreaming alone. But
this midnight I look back to the wall
where the sofa hogs its old place and the couch
is gone, like you only a few hours
of silence ago. I know I could never,
should never, have stroked your face
or stiff hair, or sat down to hold you –
Unthinkable, Phaedra or Jocasta woman!

Still, an aura of you, sulky, reserved
in thought, by now unbiddable adult being
might be said sleepily to linger around.
And it circles poor Phaedra on;
if only for a wish, the frown magicked;
if only for that tendril of the
old smile you snaked out shyly after
my shy last kisses: the scarce whisper:

'physically I am alone, touch me a little
though I'll back and hurl stones on you from
behind my rock, for I'm well aware of
Jocasta, of Phaedra and of course Medusa
O glint-haired mother – But touch me a
little, at the forking of the ways.'

Autumn in Kensington Gardens

– for Michèle Roberts

Day after day the still glitter
drifts into a ragtag of leaves
and the blackbird's bobtail
scouts among the dry heaps.

We talked, intensively
comparing, of the pale gold
of the round polled trees
all up along the Broadwalk.

What kind of yellow would
you say they bore? I have
a mist memory of the ovals,
a Kate Greenaway verse book

of cut-out leaves, each poised
for child's colouring, on its own
like prizes on the tree
in the middle of the winter dance.

Each one a glass lemon,
its yellow below its bumpy
glassy rind a tantalus
under my finger sliding by.

The hard lemon rolled
in my palm. I composed a
tree of fruit, a luscious golden
pear and a silver nutmeg.

And as for me I was
daughter to the Queen of Spain
and the curls on the head
of the gardener's girl

were as simple and red
as the herrings that grow in
the wood and as fat
round my right thumb

as the strawberries that swim
in shoals in the duck-
green Serpentine, at night,
when the gates are closed.

Children by the lake

Hi Miranda. Hi Arthur. I'm back.
They don't look.
Scuffling the moonlit gravel.
They wear picture book snow caps
red and blue with bobbles.
Studiously nattering, small as
they are.
                    What do they say?
No answer. Mirror talk?

Under ice the water's not deep.
From the air if you leaned
from your toy plane, waving
you'd see a serpentine robe
sewn into ice, edged in a rabbit's
fur trim of snow. By night
the moonbeams avert to eyes,
Alsatians in the park, lions.
On air or by air I swing by:
my skin whips and cools.
By night the robe's
softened. I round each
                    dark inlet.
Holm oak, beech, hollies
cluster like mildly
                    talking crowds.
They converse around the swathed
limbs I'm overflying.
                    Days
the glassy water lies in gaol.

I left the two children, quietly
pushing up into the air
with my feet, calf muscles
thigh muscles. Holding breath

after breath, hard bellied . . .
Once you have the knack
                      nothing to it

(or on the other hand
between one lake and the next
nothing: the skill cuts
                      of a sudden
goes missing, a whole life).

Now, from up hundreds of feet
the luminous water in gaol
becomes a rabbit doe's nest,
a loving mother's
                      languorous and
overspilling bed, surrounded
by tapestry leaves and small
lions couchant under the trees.

What are they talking about?
Their mirror chat. I let
my muscles relax like a net
so that
                      down I drop

        land
    without the least
  pricking of the gravel

        well
      with such finesse
how can they know what
      their mother was up to?

How long
I flew on high over
that melting bower, not
ruffling the leaves nor

disturbing the silver ruffed dogs
in their walk among
the moonbeams, their eyes.
In a sniff of the sound of
              your mirror talk . . .
By the freeze in the
dark your coloured caps swing
tassles, your heads nod
to each other, two
children I call my children.
How soundless you are.

Memory: glass/through which
I cannot push. The lake:
glass. I fly so high,
thankfully and coolly
I lose my mind in air.
Memory: glass/through which
I cannot push. Memory:
the robed body of the lake,
how beautiful . . . how beautiful
in her melting bower

              I dropped down
                  unnoticed
after the flight, behind children.
My children who stand prophesying
              on the gravel.

Love of babies and children

I slough each child off
every year or a couple.

I

Babies
their toes and fingers, of course perfect,
restless
helpless, but the tensile
strength coming –
The mouth
a spider movement against
my breast which is huge

We bathe in milk . . . it's the
element we share, the two of us
Her rapt bird's skull, the
skin sleek first thin plumage
My baby's whole body
held close, breathes to me
her dear perfume

And so I must too; milk
cow   But to the infant
who hasn't met
that downgraded creature
to my baby's mouth
a bird's pout

I'm wholly
the worth of warmth, of mass . . .
Rivulets, riverbrown nipples, wide yet
spraying white skeins
such as waterfalls spread out
over rocks and moss

My arms bastions to uphold

the drinker, the bird with intent eyes
sucking at each fountainhead

My shoulder a tower
to her surrender

And lastly a sound in
the beginning of darkness and sleep,
a contralto of milk   to lull

the drunken bird, a lush at her age
rose skin
                the blown skin
of, who cares?   I guard that

2

That child grows older (the
new baby comes). Our old
element stretches
between us
thinner, not without
its moments, but thinner –
                    adulterated.

The milky smell leaves
their hair slowly, then almost
from one day to the next
it's gone. You are combing
a girl or boy's hair, thick.
They pull from the comb,
complaining it's hurting
their skin.

          You suppose
they get a kind of revenge,
their own back for
an absence.

Until it fades away,
with all that complaining.
You pull them towards you.
How they wriggle away
          like snakes.

Night-time

Last night taking me
by my arse widened by
his fingers, he threw
himself into me and left
his head of knowledge
his perishable spirit
which I swallowed and
I think he died.
I was lucky and brave.
Then as I slept
she rose again in her
red negligee, a tank
of soldiers, a rose
a spread millefeuille bosom
a head of Pharoic wisdom
and she wanted not only
hers, but my (blue) negligee,
which I screamed at
since she had the wisdom
and my mother's rose.

'Will you spend today with her?'
She smiled with indifferent
certainty.
I wept, and behind her
a thin wand, a
beggar of two willow eyes
rose up aimlessly far off
from me. Rootlike
he moves to sneak back
inside. Why? What for?
He pleads with the pool to
root back his blue
ankle bones: 'you
cut me down.'
I don't want him.

Tears, they
moisten the ground.
Tears like this secrete him,
refresh his terrain.
Tears, they
moisten his ground.

Who will gun down
   the weeping willow man,
      you who are dead inside?

            Who will save me
from the willow man, the willow man?
Who will kill the willow man,
                  spirit inside?

      I'll save you from
            the willow man, the willow man
      I'll kill the wicked willow man
                  but let me come outside.

I'll give you blood, I'll give you
      back both flesh and bone
Now save me for he walks my way
            the weeping willow man

      And in the morning
      the intruder wanders over to me,
      I lay my head on him.
      Before the sun and the clock
      strike, the intruder
      wanders over to him, she
      in sleepy warmth
      lays her head on him,
      she basks
      on his mouth of roses.

Morphine

I was in a room, in a chair.
I leant forward to see the garden.
Miranda my daughter and Alec and
then Irving moved away, talking.

Some gesticulating, a conversation
rounded and cheery. I called out
things that were sociable and pleasing
from the other side of wavering walls.

Deeper inside the house I was in such
gauzed pain I had to exist
in two rooms at once. The first,
the one I leaned from, had a wall

or no wall, a window or no
window. The other I knew of
but that room was shunned, half
dark, in further, a sawn glimpse

feinting in to mazes thought
existent in the house; mere
scratches, discolourations, markings
guessed off corners polished like

tusks, but out of focus at once.
I cast my eyes back right away.
I called to the three who were
sauntering off; my remarks brilliant.

My middle-aged simpering and the
Mystery of Mr Duncan's Maiden

Giggling, simpering, ugh . . . I didn't however
see I was counterfeiting 'such Puberty'
such Mystery, the Maiden, 'the crystal clear brook'
that 'well of water we return to' . . . And I
the contaminator . . . In which for her father's loss
Ophelia ' "the little Fertility ghost" ' drowns herself;
and likewise silvery Lizzie ' "drowning for an hour
or so" posed for Millais to capture a
wild chastity' . . . Wild . . . She did drown, of laudanum.
Brooke of Lethe . . . Meanwhile, unlike Marianne
   Moore,
me again giggling and desecrator of that
inviolate field. And I thought men.

I do forget romantic men have cherished highs
about young girls who they fear to love.
' "I live in fear" ' (Lawrence). O law-flame.
You and I, old Beatrice, in our bikinis, our
parti-coloured flab, should wear grave shades
and prop by the breakwater shadow
and keep our ghettoblasters low,
our horse teeth within our lips,
no 'coy glances . . . girlish attitudes'
you, bony legs up giggling, 'loathsome'.

Reminding me all of it of abysmal
uncertainty, once

   Trying To Be THE MAIDEN

                        See how
'*lovely to look at*   Modesty
imparts to her nakedness a willowy
grace . . . Bright with spring . . .
Thus Rachel' at nine years old

'a girl, lifted to Jacob's dry mouth
her cup that fed his manhood's thirst.'
No one in my teenagerhood told me
to feed Jacob's dry thirst . . . How
did I know it was the favourite
thirst and first to feed, my own a long second?
See now, it was you . . . musing along
all the time musing along
to plague me in my fat and trenchant aim,
nervy, rapid to back down.

So that I writhed   looked aside
my neck both   Swan and Leda   *chubby*
jawline imitative best as it could duck.
And skinned myself in your eye's quest
for the willowy wild grail
within my huge girlish attitude.

Water to water, cellulose to thin air
to anorexia's grace, bulimia's modesty
'Persephone showed brightness of death
her face, spring slumbering'

Later I knew it again. That 'a wife
may be maiden to the eye', by grace
of the 'watery blues and greens' of Bonnard's
bathrooms – designer Mystery of maidens!

This shrinking inviolate
you bear such love of, I went and simpered
and spoiled it or her. And let you down.
As you and yours have done to me
and mine century by century.
Our heads forced down into a bath,
a brook, some puddle.
Muddied you say by our own wallowing.
We should lie outstretched, as
'jewels innocent show in lovely depths . . .
Because it is mystery, such Puberty

counterfeited in simpering coy glances, piety
      giggles, girlish attitudes
is loathsome, contaminated water, field
      desecrated by picnickers'

Mud in your eye, Robert Duncan.

Note: the poem 'The Maiden' is in Robert Duncan's collection, *The Opening of the Field*, 1960.

The legend of the handless queen

She has eyes like
        harebells, blue, they stare
    and mean indefinite
ecstasies. Folk say she was
    always like that, touched.
The king's son listens to
        her dumb counsel, he
    clutches her arms,
            the no handed bride,
brass coloured as ripening rye
and with gratitude for
            her clear purity, her sworn
        harebell stare, he beds
the handless queen of the rye.

Lost in a dark wood and
        searching for two children
        her babes, who float
    to the bottom of the pond
before she can cry 'no, wait!'
her stumps, groping frenziedly
        dipped in mud, grow
            slowly, muscle round bone
nerve, capillaries, skin: the ten fingers
swim like transparent roach. They
    touch her children, twine on
            their round white skulls
like weed, but to lift them.
        They gasp in her arms,
            they sick up the pond.
Her risen fingers clean their mouths and
    plant them to her.

His own hands are longstanding,
    brown, each finger
        flexible and squared
thumb pads well developed.
He has made with intricate
    sorrowing art, silver hands
        for his clear pure, sworn
bride. When she returns from
    the forest, wet and pondweed twined
        like a dead corpse
he at least can comfort her
    'your silver hands are done
        my clear bride, my one'.
She has two children clamped
    to her stumpy teats
and with her deft free hand
    throws the silver pair
        onto the roaring fire.

Scorpions in a Tuscan farmhouse

I

The scorpions come in by twos
as if to an ark, as if twining tails,
as if in the cold twilight, the end of summer
they are bored of stone, of growing colder
now in corners, and have cast
themselves as ordinary beasts
at one with the same creation
as us: unconscious they are black sores
splayed in the growing evening
on the door jamb, upside down on
the wood lintel above our entering heads.

Welcome, say the mute skull and crossbones
the dulled escutcheons
— And the *casa* teems, in its roof,
in its floor, in its woodstore downstairs
with nurseries, natural
and small as birthmarks. It takes me
all night and nightmares to rearrange
my ark and most gingerly to allow
these two only their due berth.

2

To help me you say
these two scorpions lost their way.
We go into a routine about lonely Lucifers
tied to their own tails like cans to dogs
or the other way round. There are
too many fretted ceilings to study.
Galileo would give up.

Today we are going to Camaldoli
and to see San somebody's cave, high
high before the lands slope to the Adriatic
and over the sea to Greece. I want

to get up and no further, stick
among the glowing Etruscan pines
which look soft however they scratch
squirrels. Everything is going wrong
but I rely on one thing: what I learnt
in long garish or dingy nights.
I even remember – and I want
not to do that again, but to laugh,
just as you find me (Look, behind you, a
great brown lizard, on that wall, there)
– myself literally crawling along the
corded yellow carpet screaming and moaning.

Has that to be part of my strange creation?

Has it a part? After all?
(Hiding and then advancing out like a twirler,
smiling and strychnine-happy, but damping that
down, being my happy self, *darling*?)

3

Feeble rococo! Merely I offer this:
we are both of us devil, both sunk, both have lost,
we search intensely; neither can
bear to be cause; rid it,
spray it out of our tails backward
over our shoulders. We should give each other,
shouldn't we, something more like
honey, a melting crust . . .
whatever it is the natural blessed
endow, smear yellow sweet in cruets and
make flourish in the hive . . . Our talk
is our laborious crust of honeycomb.
We hustle for simple treats and at what hour
to retract the prod . . . Can something
be made, real, that is so often,
broken, almost I'd say vigorously
and the making half spontaneous and then interrupted?

Still, you beam, the sky beams
on the house, the lizard scuds up the wall
behind a white drainpipe,
for a moment there are no shields raised,
no childhoods.
The autumn wind is softly teasing
small trees, as if we were in a fresco
grave and generous, by della Francesca.

The room is Eleanor Butler

Show them to Eleanor Butler, No. 6.
And No. 7 is Sarah Ponsonby.
You show no interest, refusing me
George Borrow, who walks Wild Wales deep
in your suitcase ravine. I say
we might never be here again, in No. 6
watching a brown mallard floating
in the big Dee of many pools
and corridors and willows midstream.
Is the duck sitting comfortably? Is she in No. 6?
Eleanor Butler, for whose sake I think
I am put up here, has three graveyards
to lie in with her Beloved,
her heart's love all their lives.
Despite what people say, they weren't mice
nor poor witch women in scuttle hats.

They adored the Gothic and twice
Wellington came to visit. They tackled
the slums, twitched away at preferments,
X for chaplain, She would prefer Y
for headmaster. They sat up in the second
ceremonial barge that glided overhead the Vale
when Telford opened his Viaduct: the
short benefactresses looking down.
Into dewy mornings they gambled. Learned
as magpies they wrote their Day Books.
The world and the Duke came riding by.

Not for his high-nosed teatime grunts
nor for the kicked-back quips they laughed at
over the fat lustre pot; nor for
that cabinet of Tighes and Piozzis;
nor for the lissom improved cottage,
their vantage from which to improve the classes.
— But for their insistence, their younger

profound insistence that flowed wide
as Wordsworth might and probably said
– that flowed wide and spread outward
like the Dee over milder ground
after its fight through hard passes –
fight to have no more and no less
than this ground: E B & S P.
– For their love I do envy them.

Over the mantel to honour the Duke's
visit; it lasts and lasts; their
modest insistence. O uneasy sleeping friend,
here's love at sixes and sevens,
love as two adjoining hotel bedrooms.
How they would have chortled
and pushed off in their barge overhead.

Note: Eleanor Butler and Sarah Ponsonby inscribed their initials over the
mantel in their Gothic Regency cottage 'Plas Newydd' in Llangollen.

A summer haze over the sea

                    I remember
you   you fucker   and the white
sea at Cuckmere Haven.

The male attendant
holds out a robe.
He gives a V sign
as the Queen of Sheba
trembly and spangly
steps from the milk of the Channel.
A two sailed ship passes:
into a broad slipway that expands
between the crescents of the water
and the clarity of sky (*that's*
the sky) . . . a light
in which horizons drift loose,
where dimensions unfasten,
a whiteness that Sheba's eye
hits with wonder, returns to
with exasperated wonder . . .
Within the collar of silver
neither sea nor sky are harnessed really at all.

Yet it broadens, broadens,
it snags in crabs, cormorants,
a ghost ship, a spirit
splashing by the water's edge.
Until the sun goes down
and she goes with him
back, trudging
over the piled shingle breakwater.

                *   *   *

Lady and playboy
they tuck into their barouche

183

of flowing silver, inside which
they instantly dispute and disagree
over anything and everything as
they skitter and rumble homeward;
once, in their heat, tipping out into
the cowfield, what with his tickling
and her poopoohing . . .
no one could claim much for this pair.

*   *   *

   Into the broad slipway
       the boat sails

A spit of rock as the tide sinks
     down   uncurls from
       the chalk cliff   like

    a dark bar of cloud
       Above   below, the slipway
a curved dazzle   loosened   far

    floating   the mast
       peters around the rock as if
       floating

from
***The Rabbit Magician Plate* (1992)**

With love, January

They are stretching out like shadows,
some of these nights. The love whose skirts
you in your last letter kissed,
I lift them for you.
Thumbelina squatting on her lily pad
writes to the swallow, because in his
smoothie lapels, nacreous tiepin, shot blue tails
soon he'll fly that 'sweet little thing'
far from – Ah, your fingers stretch longingly
over me, I'd have the odd wrong note,
·it would be luxury to say
'go slow, flier,' you winged piano man.
Or have you thinned to a mobile of swallows
by midnight, over the truckle bed, through
my aching: wood flecks?
Not so simple. I smiled, when
your letter called me all sorts of names.

Slovakia

We will love in the uncertain lift
at the Dukla, we will mesh,
we will quiver and wobble,
two lions and a cage going down.

Please, more decorous
on the high street. The cathedral
demands it, a soprano descends
the loudspeakers over the gardens
innocent and rich as snow.
It's the organist, who sings
behind her gilded machine.
Girls and women haunt
their golden Our Lady.

Coal dust burst into our room
at five o'clock this dark morning.
The cathedral walls are apricot,
its elaborate spire blackened.
A freight train passes –
thinking of your grandparents
though this train carries the brown
coal to Prague and Bohemia –

we think, entering the painted
synagogue, with its congregation
of only eleven old souls to dust
the Torah and lovingly intone
to us – yes how tall iron
stalls conveyed impurity
all the early hours north
to Poland. Your young aunts, owners
of childish faces. Thirty trucks

pushing over the road endlessly,
black gold going west
after all, in a cold evening,
teenagers waiting, whistling
by the barrier in cheap denim.

The gardener getting on

I know three evil names,
ground elder, bramble, and bindweed.
One apes roses for thorns, one strangles
while playing Angel on its trumpets,
one is less drama but comes up
stolid like tank regiments
reported out of steel roots.

My old chums (a worse pack of weeds)
crow how heavenly, a lush green riot!
Do they, I wonder, do it spitefully?
Seeing my fingers knotted and flushed?
Or to comfort? I'm not so sure.
She's near to her final ground,
our elder – is what cheers *them* up:
my rusty gold chrysanths cut-throated
and lost. Comforters, your ground
elder lives. That's the red finger
that claws down as undegradable
as plastic, I promise, to get a hold

and wrench out the evil ones.
I'm tougher: my blessed flowers
queue in the earth for their true
time of colour from the sun,
and feed from the rain gravely.
I love to work and mind this garden.
There'll be no riots, lush hellish
or green heaven. I'm more
leathery than God or Satan.

The domestic woods

– for my mother in illness

The independent cat
walks through the domestic woods by herself –
The grasshopper jumps –
Who needs a hand?
Neat and sleek as a brown
flycatcher dancing along the fence:
the picture sang.

In the mirror
suddenly the bird fell dying from the air,
the cat now lost to freedom
in rain soused fields
where tempest
felled oaks and barred paths.

A tremor
seizes the mirror of her picture –
they were saying, they were stammering –
Flying along to her
through the clouded air, bird empty cloud –
Through the wingless woods of the
bird empty air –
they were stammering, they were stammering –

Curse the oak-tree, never swear
by the oak-tree, the unfaithful,
the cat hangs in its hempen hair,
fluttering,
spilled across paths.

The passenger of the car

We flew,
myself bolt upright,
comfortable,
like an ivory duchess
on the luxurious dark blue back seats.
(The chauffered duchess
he accused
and wanted me to act up to).
I tapped his shoulder.
The dark blue chauffeur
frowning like a triton unfountained.

He drove,
hair slicked back with salt sea,
a large low forehead
furrowed like a wake,
the sweat like pearls bouncing
from his frown into his streaming eyes.

He flew
like a purring ship
through a fogbound forest.
Scrub oak: you should see
the bold dark green leaves
like children's cut-outs,
off such wisp-like trees.

The night flew
the pearl car
past a border of pearl saturated
salt-preserved mansions,
each for a duchess,
each gunned into the little oak forest,
each its own pearl.

Such flawless trim.
The cut-out leaf becomes
indefinite:
no dark nor bold leaf,
what is there
but a comb of mist sorting the hanks
of a bald and lame wood?

Because of the frailty of the trees
– I had mislaid
through tinted glass
a more precise sense of their growth –

trembling,
after much consideration

because I was frail,
because the seats were as plush as dew

at length I opened the weighty
dark blue door to the oak forest.

I flew
like a car of fog
up from the sea
and pouring inland in thick waves.

Repeatedly, repeatedly,
I tapped his dark blue shoulder.

At length, after much consideration
because I was frail,
pearl-like,
I opened the weighty door
into the low wisp-like scrub oak-trees.

Eurydice

Eurydice never died.
It was Orpheus who went down
eagerly to the city of Hades.
He walked like a bandsman
with a broad back and the slung lyre
that had charmed all living things.

Birds, animals and Eurydice
followed the singer, whimpering and pleading.
– She held up her arms,
glowing in sun
but his back was turned on her,
he lost himself in the cloak flaps
of sumptuous Persephone
who patrols the buried walls.
The mouth of the beast Cerberus
fed him down.

A venom bit Orpheus, maybe
some snaky envy of his own tongue?
At any rate he died, and
the birds, beasts and weeping woman
climbed in a sad file
back through stalactites and rock lumps
to the small high-up sun.

Eurydice hoped to die,
to join him; but instead,
seeing her white face,
which was grief, not death,
I was sorry for her
and I whispered, go to the shore.

I followed her discreetly
as her tears sprang down
on the brown and scarlet leaves.

We trudged through
a great plane-tree forest
to the sea. She took
the seashell, broken and chipped
but still iridescent
and zigzagged with amber words
as I'd set it for her;
it lay by the wave.

And that way,
pressing my shell to her ear,
bending to hear against the breaking
roar, as I'd suggested,
she heard her singer.
The dolphin and the seagull
flew from element to element
while Eurydice heard
his voice, Orpheus murmuring
marvellously from under the shore.

Under the slamming of the waves,
the young man murmuring to her:
I am here, here, my love,
in a glittering town.
I stand up in a tower,
I see all Hades –
With my lyre
I call out the illustrious beauties
of this place, the beat
and hustle of its fires, the jewel
in the small flame, sea-blue
or sea-green, Eurydice my love.

She cries
into the zigzagged shell:
Orpheus come back – you're
wrong, you're in hell,
Orpheus my love, come back.
But the shell gives out one song

whispering, ecstatic.
Each minute a wave
roars, to block it.
Eurydice walks home
through scarlet leaves
and the cracked stumps of trees.

The shell
sits by the tidemark.
I followed her ten times to
that amber whorl and ten times
her expressive eyes
said, as she bent: my love,
my agony.
I was myself hopeless and wiser.
I hurled the shell
out to sea on the autumn tide,
for the fish to crowd in
and catch the blind corpse's voice
sing of fire
and gawp and gape
in their pure shoals,
nosing for the singer.

Jacob and the angel

He flew at me like a ghost in a top-hat
but I went at him like a champ.
I doubled my fists, in my sweatband
and my singlet and long black tights
and my elastic sided pumps.

We didn't wrestle,
he carried me,
he carried me along on thin air.
He spread out his grey white wings
like a swan or a goose or an aeroplane
aloof on miles of solid air
and I his underbelly, his breast, his fuselage
held like the under half of a clam-shell.

Pluming me in my body
as heavily as a feather or
the believing finger of a tornado,
the angel carried me along under him
by this finger, I holding to it,
upholding him like an intelligence of air.
We didn't wrestle,
the wrestling was over,
this comrade beat and thundered and whispered
inside me with his breadth and length
whispering, my Jacob, my main man, my woman.

Poor weather

At dawn, rounding the head,
the water a flat calm, and then storm
brushing in, veiling in.

Spray pushes and pushes on the breakwater,
utterances opening and continually
fasting on stone and ending,

rambling onto stone and ground,
sipping in estuaries
through tunnels slanting back deeply.

Yellow flag for cowards like me,
he turns back, tethers his delicate dinghy,
the wind expending on the bay,

and gracefully drinks of his daring
in the florescent pub that evening.
The boat urges itself on its mooring.

September, Kerry

At three waking and looking
                    through floral curtains
the hurricane gale's bled out
the sea's barracking and quaking
                    the stones merely
and a stiff penny face the moon stares hi
travelling at the full and at a standstill
her Indian yellow coiffure, her
                    gasoline aureole
turning round on the cloud crust
                    never burning –
Stare to the pack below, wolves in the bay
                    restless and snappy
or white hares
      their long ears flared and sprayed back
as they breast in, smartened by the moon.
But later I want to lie down, to sleep,
      burrow into the undercut of dark mountains.

The Earl of Modern Ireland

All billowed to noble queenly or
   kingly size,
beeches, copper or green, sycamores,
limes, oaks too, though elms
   have gone since.

Cromwell's man's desmesne;
   the grass: stinking green lush.

Jackdaws: clack and flutter-tumble –
   Spider servanted, jackdaw butlered
– It's a mercy the whole place doesn't burn
down in a chimney fire one night
while His Nibs is in Dublin, London.
   Others have.

Whee – here comes the mist
   up from the lake, breath and arms
     urging out of the wetlands.

2

Blue-eyed Euro-farmer Michael

                   'one moisty
morning at dark-eyebrowed five, in the darkness,
I drive up to collect my cows for market, load
them, go on to the next place where I have
stock, and impatient to see not a light,
the farmer snoring, cows moving dark in the
farmyard. Ah hell. A figure in the dark darkness
looming, it's Father in his dark black cassock
all in the dark and wringing his hands eleven
times, we're in terrible terrible trouble but
somehow unable to spell out the trouble.
Weeping the farmer who keeps my herd runs

shouting and his wife weeping and the little
children weeping and he jabs me in the chest
with his shotgun in lessening dark and jabs
and jabbers, I can't take it any more, I'll do
away with myself, prodding me with the barrel
and Father in darkness dancing by willing but
helpless – Off my heart I pull the barrel of
the shotgun, the farmer yields it up sobbing
and I uncock it, unload it and now to me the
greying light announces my beautiful champions,
my mothers all in calf, £70,000 worth so I'm
telling you after dinner in the firelight in the
library, and the farmer, God's Act of a
betting man, has for the bookies sold 34 cows
in calf while I was away in Australia'

                as he stands the backs of his
thighs before the red logs among the fragrant
leather of His Lordship's great 18th Century
library, 34 cows you'd not miss at a glance in
a herd of 400, in a herd of 73 in rising sunbeams
out of the dark of the night there would be bound
to show a little lack.

3

His Lordship to give a lecture
at Ballynamuck, on the French landing.
He has no notion where or when
or who to ring or who rang him
                in the first place.

At lunchtime on the day invited
Ballynamuck rings, they're having
a Mass for the dead and stone blessed
and no lecture. Himself gives hearty thanks
              and stops swotting.

On the grassy lake at the walk's end
lives the lady of the lake
and her white spouse the bull swan
and one grey maiden, whimpering.

To the food island orange with lilies
came to her five brothers and sisters one night
a mink: that swam beneath them one by one
and bit off and made off with each sleeping head
and left the five corpses floating
and now she whispers up and down all day.

Fiddle de dee of the young trees . . .
The Earl is obsessed with slurry.
Sued for polluting the river
he instructs Messrs. Murphy not to appeal
against that scocious trout-fishing magistrate:
'. . . in my fifty years on the bench'

Mr Murphy puts in the appeal.
His Lordship's fine is doubled.
De profundis of the full-uddered oak-tree . . .
Cows full-uddered, moving and swaying
muck-arsed, paper labelled and rubber docketed,
one being on each side of her black face
branded 20 in satin white hair . . .

His Lordship's Folly

He brings her
to bed

He brings the youthful stream
to her new bed, to her bolsters
of day-lilies and hart's tongue.

He rejoices her

He rejoices his bride with bluebells
and to the embrasures of great roots
he devotes the primrose.

<table>
<tr><td>He adorns the way
with bugloss and
other flowers</td><td>Make diamond the bride's path
through bugloss, through ragged robin.
Let her run through conifers.</td></tr>
<tr><td>She caresses him</td><td>He builds her a foolish island
full of amethysts and orchids.
She holds it in her arms.</td></tr>
<tr><td>He dresses her
in gold</td><td>Boned by an inlay of mosses,
corsetted by the gold quatrefoil,
the stream glides to her dress.</td></tr>
<tr><td>And she takes him
to her</td><td>Like a wizard he has struck her
with his wand and he has called
and she flows on all his sides.</td></tr>
</table>

7

The tourists come, stepping gingerly.
They have paid their pound –
for slurry and the primrose?

Through a leafless rhododendron
they press on and here are swans!
Vikings on the water

mink slain, dignified, eaters of algae,
children of the Vikings on the lake-water
beating tempestuously –

8

Skeletal forms do not pester His Honour,
never hit him in the boyish face
like bats loosed out of their cave
by someone's indecent mistake.

So he is lucky – the State of the Nation
is fairly fat and European
and for each Anglo master of plenty
no longer a hundred go dying.

Such luck! And why so forgiven?
They pay their pound in money
of the mint salmon of conservative
Irish wisdom: which gives him the place.

9

In the event of victory, hold on to your
rifles, as those with whom we are fighting
may stop before our goal is reached. We
are out for economic as well as political liberty.
Hold on to your rifles.

James Connolly to his Citizen Army
before The Rising, 1916

Song of the Bull and Cow Rocks off Kerry

The sea horn swings, swings the sea tail
                sea udder sways

Out beyond seagulls
               hump, skip Bull and Cow
Other side of the mist yard, far small
        in Atlantic water meadows
      bellow the black Bull and the black Cow

Sea udder sways, sea horn swings
                swings the sea tail

Feudal

– from Bresson's Lancelot du Lac

A child is tying brushwood –
        whisking like a blackbird
  head
      feathered on its lightning stem
    eyes glimmering in starved skin
whiten
       like a horse hauled up to halt
              in the wind

Out of the wood   out of the wood
        he states: I've lost my way –

Leaves break at the shoulder
             of the charger
    at a leg's cylinder dangling
      crooked in chain mail
This is Escalot – the crone replies

After the wound her mother's curing
     their hovel   he dying   she
    hunched   the girl eternally
    scuttling   for ever bringing in
                 kindling!

he heads off on the enormous
      castle flanked   star headed bay
           she scuttles this time
          to seal the last hoofmark
with kissing

She like a squire had stored
              the armour
His blood clotting like a villein's

His eye far from
                eagle   wolf   man
slitting and slamming the glades from
                    the palanquin
    of the stratospherical horse

    Eye   far   not starry white
                                        ablaze

        Mind curing in the candle

God's tongue – the lance   God's cloud –
                        the shield, casque!
        The ton weights for me carried
    by the sweet lord, O merciful Lord!
in whose protection from those giants
                    straddling   axing the woods

as they themselves fall to one another's fury
    – whatever their rammed weight catches

He in whose protection   I am
        a white pebble   a soul saved

He picked me up, then out of the thicket
                        came
        a wild boar   with an iron snout
                    – a white stare
Lord Jesu they lifted up on the gallows tree

Kissing the plate-like prints
            of a giant horse
            Before its sallies and courses
                        stones fly

    each clover obeys
    not with its root, but with its green stem

Pandora Armistice

Pandora rich as Midas but nowhere so mean
sits by the step each day and sells her flowers.
For free this street-seller allows you to dip in,
pushing the basket forward when you gulp, Ready!

You know how the regiments can fly up in sheathes,
but death can fan from a head of deranged pistils.
You must edge round these clusters, and the blooded mash
of poppies, and fainting lilies, and stalks fixed like bayonets.

You must poke your fingers past the flowers of the grave
and hook free the layers of dolls lying underneath,
yellow and brown dolls and black and ivory
done up in rows of gauzy gold and silver.

Free them and they'll fly up like fishes
and make their commune between her breasts like peonies
and like bees ride into her armpits
like foxgloves, and like butterflies into the tulip

of the earth blooming, the bulb giving forth
her calyx of husk, light, honey, salt.
Through her treasures white poppies slide and slip.
We all died. It was all nonsense. We should have lived.

Generations

A distressed mother rejects another
distressed mother rejects
another distressed mother rejects
another distressed
another

another   another

tries to heal the sore place
deep   under layers of
hard sharp wound tissue

hard

Sylvia Plath's grave, Hepdenstall

                              A thick
waved slab, mottled grey,
regulation end-paper.
A yard of grass
tight-lips this dead will.

What orientalism, what wealth
has been drummed up
on this skinned ridge.
Mud, harrowed back, fresh.

On stage are more
garrulous tombs, black
and shining with fear of death.
Minutely dated, nothing spared.

Even amidst fierce flames . . .
the lotus may be planted . . .

I lose the words, among
spidery rain falling on thin top-soil.

Even amidst such flames
herself she dusted down to this
cleaned out grate.

She governs me
with her still furious flowering –

Therefore, her steely horses
proceed, ice white
white heat –

Sisyphus who was Prometheus

Sisyphus thinks it's a crappy job, oversleeps.
Night and dreams divert him and take his attention.
Illuminated by a wet dawn
the boulder moves lightly up the mountain.
Moss grows, soft as a cat stepping.

*   *   *

Bald, a tonsil in throat dark.
Once again Sisyphus sleeps in
the monster's dusk, run off his feet.
All day all day go on go on yes yes nearly
But not – Omigod you motherfucking

*   *   *

Temple of Demeter configured
of marbles, limestones, clays, gemstones, granites.
Where the cycad roundly untongues above
the mirrorless beetle, lizard's dropping eye
and ratchet lichen. Greatly it rains:
green grows the conservatory; with inside
fogs netting and beading the red herring-boned
tiles, pipes, spiral stairs, cliff-faces,
tree-crowded hilltops, panes,
drop herding to drop under the stratosphere.

No column, no pediment. It worked out
like a cat quartering a hillside speechlessly,
moving up or down with intent.

*   *   *

What's happened to fire? From the above dank
and homely symbiosis, he comments, the sun
has been totally excluded. Sisyphus swears,

211

in God's vent he found something unparalleled,
that wasn't before and can't be again.
Making a straight line for it.
Thing unrepeatable, far more than earth grain
or liquid drop: a flicker he saw come
once and to infinity, one and one and one
along oil or coal or wood edge.
He saw its edges and where the next
ringlet or wave came into its own life.
Therefore make a central place for his straight
capture; nothing clanks round for ever
without a motor. How forlorn
to fear and to give the fire-carrier
this boulder-peddling to mock his fierce grasp.

*   *   *

How can he allow a single water-drop
to run down, a mere stone to find its own level,
he who has climbed his brains for fire
as I have, has timed it, his heart beating
for the whoosh, each occasion with such work
to the crater's edge, detonation after detonation.

How can I allow a bare stone day after day
to lose its balance and to finish up
in the same trough? Nothing can climb
this hill without me. Day after day
I am crushed with the duties and the sadness of God.

The selfish one

Is this selfish, the stoat
that charmed my ribs, the way my knees
unpin for the mother of pearl wrench . . .
Kneeling . . . Yes, she sees it so.

— To be that marble pippin
twirled, teazed by tongue and teeth!
Integument crisp, acid sweetly
she'd lay hands on, and not

peck to a scab, whistling,
or, as a tree past bearing,
slap the apples, thump,
even the ones unripe, to the four winds!

This a minute ago; around
itself the minute makes a film
as a raindrop proofs itself to rain.
Then one flood, three decades crystal.

Inside the flood an apple
sank down, saturated, and the
pip fruited into the flood bed,
fully possessed with the liquid

of bearing. And therefore the fruit
better rinded, not against lions
and tigers, not against the stoat
of love: against thievery of flesh,

against pecking, against calluses of
careless let-fall. Rise, O lady
of longing. What long flowing
to bear and grow a selfish tree.

Brooklyn walls

— Many Egyptian, Hellenic, Aztec,
Renaissance, and made of paper.
The gritted tar-paper adorns the little shack.
Stone fortifications rear on the might
of Blois, its rubbled and dimpled blocks.
Their hills rise to battle slits or slog up
to a cottage gable and dormer
perched fifty, a hundred feet, overhead,
or plod merely to hulk. Pale blood-coloured temples
step up slashed with bone chips, nerves
and the white titbits of marbles and limestones.
Pediments gable and gargoyle,
gothic, regothic, barothic and rococo,
imprint with prolonged texts, man high,
the easy to read names in passing of Plato to Jay Gould.
Upheld by pillars like bridge stanchions; or
they guard the single mansion, dumpy
as bottle palms. Pillars to sit on earthquakes:
lonesome, or Delphic groves of threes, fours,
yard Doric, Ionian by the metre, Corinthian
bits stuck out and grape swags in heaps.
To walk a block, ceramic porch floor tiles in
grass green, sky azure, crazy Mediterranean pathways.
Each side, fountains of polymer, water frozen
in the hose tap. Upstairs the stars cut diamond
cold by night and Santa yells in fibreglass
as big as real, popping his bulbs across
the mackerel shingles of the adorned shack.
Bigger than real, in fact, and bopping along
brighter and faster than anyone else's
speed of light dare rock around the block.

The big heart of Brooklyn is red, red.
Expansive red or roan, pepper and salted,
liver and salmon and raspberry and mulberry;
also banana, lesser caramel, treacles, cringing

beiges and demolished greens, the curtain
of Giant who lives here? Black poodles
live in the castle. Hoarse and vivacious, voices
in lobbies complain of snow and fixed wealth.
The horizon stands stoic.

These are the red cliffs of the Navy Yard blocks.
Here the poor live hole by hole, like puffins
or sand swallows or troglodytes or the poor;
hole by hole though the burrows are square,
twenty stories up, a table, TV and chairs.
Unpedimented, ungargoyled, these red cliffs
of Fort Greene were built for southern Blacks
to come make World War submarines.
A large chunk of Brooklyn's red heart
since those days, unchanged; not a corner
even for a swatch of paper sidings
(grey and creamy chiselled to stone of Blois)
to take off the edge and impart style;
here are people with strong backs to walls
roach and rat riddled, here are people
who joke and shout and skate to the stores
on sidewalks of smashed bottles, garbage of stars,
diamonds for the ladies; here
are the carriage and kitchen quarters
of the castle of Giant Who and the poodles.

New England fall, by freeway

Swinish cars include us
blundering and panning across holyland.
Translucent on rocks the stained glass oaks,
the maples, bless the drivers impartially
who do or don't give a monkey's
for what our six mean streaks replaced
nor for these great survivors of the carnage
now bitted and bitten back each side
by – yes! us! the creative lords!

Between their blue leads, the weighty
laterals of spruce, cedar and pine,
these stained glass scenes in the lives
flick by us – the jewel box clerestory
mixed up with grand episodes of the nave.
We're in such glut, storming Maine to Boston.
We see no soul but blurred types –
that bend rose or golden heads.

When I was a child these crowds
sang in spheres, sometimes.
Such crowds, halleluia makers upside
down in real gold leaf on an apse
or spread etiolated and gigantic
over a transept arch, both pillars,
and coming on high to a Christ or
dove or to a flying prayer of ten fingers
lined up like palings, or better,
like ten silvery pale saplings of birch:
birch alive in a forest,
lifting themselves year by year,
generation by generation,
in praise of what I praise too . . .
as we zap on through: their land.

Inside the acute white noon
maples and oaks oscillate, the dulcet
and bristling jump of light: orange, orange,
crimson. My eye is the harpooner; but better,
the whale harbouring into its eye-mouth
the lights of the floating world.
Sap fails: to this looking-glass eye
middle radiances flow from the tree instead,
the inner molecules break outwards
along the branch, twig and stem line;
they surge the dykes of leaf veins and ribs;
all brim, then light gliding
away over the levees, the heart
pours in reds and yellows through the limbs,
the lapping outwards of waves through
five-pointed or seven or three-pointed hands,
the tree burning,
as timed for light as oil and a wick.

3

Turning the street corner the sugar
in the maples, the sap syrup,
melts on the glance in lemon sherbets,
in wine gum leaves, in wine
splattering and pooling into banana gold
five-lipped offering saucers.

As one cloud will shine like a snowdrop,
maples conquer the street for light;
clouds of golden or pink powder waved
out of a puff, out of a bedroom window
and hanging along the air at moments.

At intervals maple leaves dress
bodies with steady volcanic interiors.
They shed such starlight, endurance,
lordliness, a gas jet . . .

Lightshades, layered horn jerkins,
chain mail in rose doré, orange
bird god cloaks, the glass mantles
we had once for gas . . .

In Boston
        in Marlborough Street
                        in October
when evening comes by my window

why light the lamps?

Railroad station

All life is little railroad stations,
he murmured as he bent over her
like the older Gary Cooper, to say
goodbye; though he wore no hat,
no soft hat. Then he hitched up his
dun-coloured Brooks Brothers suit
over his furry stomach – how
she would miss nosing her way up
or down his furry stomach. Sure,
she answered under the low cirrus
dun-coloured in the orange lights
of the platform, all's arrival and departure; looking just as wan as a
girl in a film still set in Minnesota.
Still, she blew a kiss or more
as the train ranted out, on its way
to connections she with her single
'55 Studebaker did not aspire to
(he was the worldly guy); and felt
her thin hair drawn back
in the starlight into a pony-tail.

Departures are worse, she thought
suddenly, acidly, in the station –
master's torch's gleam and regretted
he'd gone, she'd like to have called
that last thing, just on the hoot
of the train and seen, as he'd bent
to light up his pipe in the carriage,
his eyelids flicker in the glow.

The Death of General Custer

– programme on American Public Television

The man. The myth. The sombre
mystery. Of the last stand.
Will we ever know? Probably
not. Exactly. Till the end of time.
Linkman explores the headstones
of the warriors of West Point:
his tanned face and grey thatch
intelligently and somberly pause in the afternoon.
So many buried . . . Yet
General Custer's fame everyone knows.

His tombstone's as high as a Cheyenne's eye.

Infant or old, bones into wide grit,
the panned grit of the fast rivers –
the bones go like a flood into the soil,
one with the dog bone, one with handfuls of chicken bone
one with turkey bone, deer bone, Indian bone
distributed like fertilizer.

Earthly flesh, infants sky-high like round birds off
the arms of breastless women
opening their mouths to

out of the arms of headless women

out of the screams of the bugle,
its shrill melancholy still plays for us
safety and rescue in our hearts and minds.
Like fluff blown up before the horse hooves
the bloody parts of newborn babies rise, rise up

kneel down before the troopers, rise up before their bullets
and kneel down before the scream of the advance.
Weeds are chopped back,
the Nations are herded to the fast river by

that tricky mystery, that dandy, that
perpetual enigma of our history, brilliant strategist:
who got himself killed and America's first defeat.
By hard assembly of bullets used,
ballistic experts have worked to show the
exact spot of the tragic fall.
Now I, linkman
and my friend the acute East Coast scholar
advance to the Bighorn question:
— General? Was it here? Or there?
Or down in the valley or halfway up
or for sure standing yellow-haired flourishing
his sword on the hill?
But exactly. We'll
probably never know till the end of time. How.

Linkman, your tones
behind my ear dot perfume
of the nation's old blood stench;
because the people dare not build a tomb
as high as a white man's eye
to the hundred thousand infants
whom Custer hated, whose
bird bones cry
inside the trumpets of the nation.

Seeing everything

– in the Sculpture Garden and the
National Gallery of Art, Washington

A butterfly going down Washington
passed me and the Calais burghers,
ignored Song and chose to rest
on the Indian woman who dozes like a mesa,
whose lap is like a hanging valley,
a massive worker taking her own time finally.

The butterfly – its own image drifted down:
a sky plane trail lost low –
in an unknown tongue made a golden remark
against the black velvets of Miro commas,
some offer of irresponsible do-nothing
I refused as soon as saw.

I see everything in the city: finally
the conquering light behind Rembrandt's mill.
But lastly, his baggy eyes say lustrously
to me – me! Why this world?
Why continue in these flat lands?
Why suffer so at the foot of the sky?

I tried to brush by; no luck, and worse,
he was three hundred years dead, with
that look, and I have the tenure
and none of the skywise gift
of the golden and black insect, and
I was talking of my despair and listening,

blind and dried, to these glossy pigments:
dreams of the large eyes and kind face
of Mynheer Rembrandt once, who told me
after a while to go back and try again,
like a butterfly, like a woman worker.

Towards nightfall, Arizona

Birds take turn on the pate
of the saguaro, swapping riffs and ruderies.

Within its body, entering and hopping,
flicker, screech-owl, finches

two or one, are pillowed on water,
nested from the crystal cold,

cooled from the sun's rocket.
In six o'clock shadow hoboes

with stove hats, pipes ahoy,
hitch-hiking arms and a bad case

of jokes – You can't get there from here –
trot on the rose-red canyons:

I'm no beggar and no god (a spiny snug,
green-skinned, boot-capped, soft-

centred, abnormally tall, blurry
on the height and visible for lives.)

Rotted, lamed on the sill of cities,
a dumb-sign: Slow down.

I keep your desert.

Note: the flicker is an American woodpecker.

223

The turquoise rabbit magician plate

At that eatery that was starred highly
and the mesquite outside burnt
with columned and pre-praised perfume
but nevertheless the smell handled me,
though now metallic and lateral jaunts
through climates later I forget:
O magician I cautiously bought whole
– Oh with what care I brought it back
and the glancing smell of your feathered spine
and trumpet, the amateur hooked back curtains,
the glaze – My own eyes I can feel
as whole, owlish, hazel, as randomly spotted –
How did men invent you – O sir, a woman!
Nothing is whole. At this last moment

distinct and concerted,
your lumpish sky, starred, your black
childish musical instrument playing rapidly,
an Apache woman painted this in tradition.

The Florida swamps

In the up-current the heron places its breast
    as plump as the wind
        abreast of a white schooner

    – the hollow-boned and feathery model
a surgeon makes of balsa spars,
        an eye surgeon whose hands

invade and exquisitely alter
      minute territories and seas

– as the red prop-roots of the mangroves
    lance and clean scour the sea
  and loop stitch its many islets around here,

over and over stitches
        along the water hem
  or along the cuff and hem of an island –

which is cut so badly, ruined by rib roots,
    as you stare in, looking for a centre,
  any idea of a self to this swamp:

    the self is historic only, to be seen
looking down a black pupil
      which expands and you see

to the back country past the lens, and there
  a comatose flicker, the past continuous
    chilling your brain, played over

   and over again, the old movie, old movie
to sickening exhaustion, no start,
    no finish, a white full-winged

heron lights on a mangrove, a candelabra
   taller, only a bird's leg taller

than a billion others (the ants,
            the bees of the swamps).
   There too a loggerhead turtle

swims along in the current, lifting out,
            lifting its jaw perodically, like
   an old boy mumbling sunshine.

                    2
            Feeding on wealthy and lavish rot
inside cocoa brown and bottle green shallow

the mangrove forks the sea,
   smoothes, slowly bursts, hatches into
               its third element, the sunny air,

then through the air it curtseys out hoops
            back to the stare of the sea; engineers
            a crinoline to lift up its

scrawny grey waist clear of the salt.
   The new island is sewn into the sea.
            Seas fill, maps after all exquisitely alter.

                    3
The Seminoles hunkered down here, forced off
   earth by repeating armies,
            hanging on in stilted shelters.

Only to them, or beggared whites – or to
   herons, ibises, spoonbills – you suppose
            the tall upbranching tree becomes a flame

of its kind, and present continuous
   rubs and salts down in their palms
            into usable strips,

jars, pots, hollowed out skiffs and thatch
    for the roof, to which known currents
        bring them swirling home

        or else they are swirled out past the
mythic and historic island of
    the gathering of the wind-breasted spirits –

way out to the islandless ocean which is
    an end and placeless.

4
But your attempt to find land
    where there is no land but
        merely islands bottomless with sea

or your attempt to find sea
    where there is no sea, no horizon
    but merely lakes inland

where there is no land
    but roots kneeling on roots bedded
        on the corpses of the lavish water

in which fish can be nursed, and oyster –
    shells are wheedling scalpels to
    flesh and foot and leg, and snakes linger –

the drain, the sink-hole
    in short, of the United States, into which
        the losers were stuffed –

it still is a blind green iris to you –
    Yet how the whole
        operation replays later

with gestureless and changeless
    blindfold and lilting vision and consolation
        long after your own eye

has caught in far off dazzle the first/last
　　　marker post, the out finally,
　　　　　as if that uniform grey chainsawed

　　wood oblong were the first outpost
on the suffering edge of the eye, of reason and sense.

Dusk and a Portuguese man o' war

We are in the tropics. I'm sorry to say
    what slews round the corner
is no fun: winningly, slidingly
    under its indigo puff sleeve
under its beacon blue eye, its arms
    outspread to me.

The lengthening sea is a sapphire sore.
    Radiant glitter: a bloom
on the face of Gabriel. But this is
    barely healed surface tissue,
reams of plastic recoiled and recoiled
    round diabolisms.

Stir it up with the spoon of the breeze.
    I remember Coleridge's sailor's
jig; the fires pivoting round the hull
    some day or night or not-light,
a stationary process. This is
    to be afraid of the least touch.

Henny Penny on another day

And again the sky above us,
Henny Penny was heard to say another day.
Contemptuously the animals
told her to shut her beak,
stop her nagging. Rocky Cocky tiptoed
high and touch-tested the sky – it's OK,
he growled – folding his wings after
a short affirmative grunt: It's hard,
and well above us, it'll never fall,
a good stiff wodge of carbons, CFCs,
nitrates like that. Pass the bottle.
He drank, beer streaming down his wattles;
the sea mouthing into the farmyard puddles
through the five-barred farm gate
into the troughs, stalls, pens, pond
in the corner; but Cocky Rocky stood
on the dung-heap in the steaming rise
of gases, crowing Gung Ho To You,
as fit as a king, as a fiddle.

Note: in the traditional tale (which ends in the jaws of a fox) Henny Penny claims
the sky is falling and Cocky Locky and others give advice.

Smart

I opened our smart casement.
Down half a mile in the forlorn lands
there a two year old girl stands,
covered with mud, wavy brown-haired, chubby,
red on her forehead, on her mouth
                                        chin, neck
as if she's been dipping into jam
and her hand will be smacked for it.

On those roads
dust crouches in the marshlands
                                in the mountains.
There appear whole new dunes in the desert.

In the cloud's abdomen
I open wide one more time,
not now for the drift down of bombs.
Clumsier today, it's packed lunches
labelled hastily with my sincerest wishes
I lob to the reddened child:
chewing-gum, beef in barbecue sauce,
                                other comforts.

Note: in March 1991 after the Gulf war the US Air Force airlifted spare
food from US Quartermaster Corps to Kurd refugees fleeing the Iraqi Army,
after an abortive uprising encouraged by President Bush. Not long
previously the Allies had been 'indicting installations' throughout Iraq,
including Iraqi Kurdistan.

The neighbors in Florida

Hey presto, Jackie popping
a brawny white-haired head
gloomily over the fence:
Hi! Come swim with me!

I've envied from my side
a pool, a fjord, an ocean . . .
It turns out four strokes up
and two of them down, and sink.

Immaculate-haired she chats
and coasts in her rubber ring:
'D'you remember New Jersey?
The exact shape of this pool!'

Her waving palms are sawn.
They browned and sank and died
of the Lethal Yellowing.
Down here we're living scared.

Jackie explains, the sun
is cancerous and huge
so we shut our door in May
and open it up in Fall.

We breathe with A/C on
indoors all summer through
and we bring up our wheelless bike
to work out by the bed.

We drive to get the stores
twice weekly at Wynn Dixie
and we chill the Buick hard
just like a Jersey spring.

And then at Sunday noon
to Pronto on the Rocks,
they do a terrific brunch
if you don't mind Donald Ducks.

She floats me down a gin:
You guys will love it here
just the way we do!
She bops inside her ring.

Night in the parking lot of El Rancho Motel

Two muscular toms, twin ginger.
One squats upright outside the wheelcap.
One, leg outstretched, eye swung,
inquires the bumper, star spangled.

Laid on a feather of the dark palm,
a moon trembles, a minute crescent,
the salver of a weighing scale.
Crickets beat tin spoons.

Unreachable under the chassis
of the silver car, holed up for how long
a smoky and creamy she-cat
lies at ease and licks her forearm.

Bounty

Drawing curtains of a simple French restaurant
the cashier spins dimes to the poorhouse opposite.

At such ratios one may lounge in attractive disarray,
ringed hands. One admires the effect wryly, then fast

aerobically, turns from the mirror smilingly;
having been brought up in schools not to be vain.

To accept, yes. With God lost in space one must seek
to love self. Half the heart knows itself, devourer,

the other ventricle pumps little amounts through
the system, to keep the toes and fingers twitching,

for working when required. The brain, that is to say
the proprietor, needs to take on help in the high season.

Mrs Bai

– for Carolyn Forché

A young woman squats in her doorway
in the sand-floored alley
outside the iron-ringed factory.
Her six month old sleeps in folds
of her sari of apricots and gold.
Her husband died of lung related
diseases last year, and before him
his father, and their daughter of six.
She waits for compensation.
She is ringed by debt.
The factory is surrounded by junk.
What manager will not throw away
a cog-wheel blunted, dull and bent.
'I get dizzy if
I try to pick up more
than three buckets of water.'

What the doctor orders

But doctor, there are innate properties
I think. How in the tropics in April
the heat's growing, not any psychic fever
but inside the balloon hot air is pumped in
daily, and more of it tomorrow, replacing
the trick or treat breeze. I want
that wind like a lollipop. I look for it
down the street as I blunder, remembering
the angles that bounce the draughts off the sea.
I rely on skin licks of yesterday and not
only on twinned eye and skin which squint
and prick for shade. But that most of all
I am wading in the dense, denser balloon
which is pressing in, not stretching, so that
I myself am the thrumming skin.
At this point I'm frightening myself again,
you say. Merely, as I look ahead,
my heart in double beats, I want the man
who is ahead of me, and taking no blind notice
of the sun. I think it is so huge
it is a flap, invisible. It is slicking him down
in front of me, he is becoming a shimmer.
And you will say, I have pulled this skin
over my head, contracted, forcibly wrinkling,
and what I must do is open and let the heat swim in!
What I must do! I want to be cool.
There are climates in this world
with their own extremes. Perhaps this shimmer
will turn around and come to me and ask.

The avocado tree

You are sweeping the avocado leaves
                              off the decking.
I am thinking in bed, just on my waking
                              but this can't be fleshed out.

Not so quick, not so easily, but one season
                              when your little house
has baptised itself for its hundredth year.

In the ferocity of April sunshine:
leaves all night-time scuttling
                              down the tin roof
and these gutter canoes (in a day's downpour)

give branch to the tuberous flower –
                              abyss yellow sea-stalk –
as you might find waving far below you.

The wind

– for I. W.

       Well, a tree
noisy in the breeze, wood yawing
but not under painful pressure, just
the opposite. And, a wind. Masses of leaves
swelling but not rushed off
in the other direction but into the wind,
into the cave of the four hundred mahout winds
trumpeting and trumpeting. And then,
to insist the blossomed tree into the source,
the caveman's fire, the warm belly
of the elephant mountain. But this is not
to fall or burn but to offer, love and have
my pleasure in the porterage of the wind.

The American woman at the ruins of Tikal

The afterword of dawn rain
is talking its way down through the leaves

at the beginning of the poem.

One hummingbird, present and not present,
in a wide glade entranced with crickets,
crickets like a city telephone exchange,
like a hand pressed down on a car horn,
like pigs grunting.

With orchid eyelids
serpents walk on thrones. They nurse
giants with eyes like grindstones,
with teeth like tank treads –

In the heat of the afternoon
they lay papaya and heads
on altars higher than the highest mahogany.
'The beautiful jungle is so friendly,'
chants the American woman on her way
up to the moon,
to the next part of the poem.

On her way up to the moon
a fly made of green marble, a frog with pink hands,
tell her, you are safer than a street here –
She springs up in old sneakers,
bean necklaces and her skirt
strange with buttercups and daisies –

On the third step of the poem
if she climbs without chanting,
she'll meet the cat o' the forest,
a fox in orange light
mothering its three stumble-pawed cubs

with a frown of yellow eyes
and forepaws like a vase, long stemmed –
Ix Ch'up, Young Moon Woman –

Dead eye, spit in your eye,
the altars shoot for the same old identical
blood-red sun, a sitting head across
the vast and transient repossession of the leaves,
ruffling and squawking.

– If the voices surround her, the spider monkeys
considering their slow high wires
a hundred feet into the ceiba tree,
and the toucan making a small streak
in the white cloud like an ibis, but
the yellow half of her is all mouth –

The moon beginning to ride
the shoulders of the poem like a silver backpack
is a weight she wants to carry off
in her arms, if she carries on praying hard
out of her unguarded forehead
and curls sweat-blackened –

Climbing down,
feeling the ringing darkened road
to the campsite: halfway,
the black and red-haired coati mundi
stands its ground, replacing
its paw on a leaf silently;
and stringing its back like a bow
it lopes to her

like a comma in a long ending sentence
as it curls to the heart
of a dark but light remembrance

(as she spreads her skirts out
in a glade that smells of deer and jaguar)
and it lays its dark light triangular head,
its light head, its yellow
and triangular eyes
in her lap of bromeliads and orchids,
on the last lap of the beautiful
and the friendly poem of buttercups and daisies.

The tourists

Who are the tourists?
One sits, writing his postcard at a window
in Quito, before the big procession.
The city is wet and white and grey,
full of Indians from the mountain
to watch the stories of the Great White God.
The Spanish priest complained, once,
the Indians have no word for guilt,
they had to be taught   guilt
This is Jesus de Mucho Poder
                    Good Friday's Man.

Leaving the table

– for Harold Pinter

You told me
what he had told you in the evening
at supper in Managua
– what they did to one man –
I forgot his name, his importance
– he was someone fairly important –
His body was found on a hillside,
hacked up, with the genitals
stuffed in its mouth,
that they did this to women,
to their breasts following rape.
That he'd lost priests, catechists, health
workers, professionals of various kinds,
as well of course as the thousands
of peasants, campesinos, campesinas.
That my kindly
America has funded such
art out of the City of Despair?
Out of Gehenna? Can I believe
in any of this – something
I dreamed up that you breathed
to me malignly over the table.
Yes but we had left the table,
and illegally wandering,
we came to a hillside where
the great folk of the city
ordered the bleeding
and the dismembering of their servants
the many poor –
those who'd said: No more.

Nicaragua and the old man in the white house

Over the mountains, over the sea
there freedom lit the morning star
and grew the flower upon the tree.

Oh well armed thieves in the night came leaping,
they slit the throats of children sleeping.
Oh who has armed the thieves so well?

A buzzard, a jackal came over the hill,
one circles, one sneaks, each to a child,
the beak and the tooth are handsome steel.

Over the mountains, over the sea,
oh who has armed the thieves so well?
Feather of steel and hair of steel.

The bird and the beast came over the hill,
they came to the house all shining white,
we've done your bidding, we've done your will.

Old man, old man, the children are dying
over the mountains, over the sea.
Smile, old man, for many are crying.

In dark he smiled, in night he smiled
and dark fell on the morning star
and wrapped the land in mourning bands.

Smile, old death, or shout or rage
but still by mountain, still by star
the growing child shall come of age,

the growing child shall come of age
over the mountains, over the sea.

Temple of the Codz Pop
at Kabah in the Yucatan

A huge iguana is the pediment
(suddenly look up and there it is, lounging).
One mask above three hundred rain god masks
ogling with their Puuc double vowels
and their boxed eyeballs the flat-winged
skeletal-stemmed acacia forests.

Red earth, laden with lacy fern leaf
where the Mayan children and thin
chocolate brown pigs and big red-wattled
turkeys walk.

Inland sea-skin, sea ripples baked
as the desert: the biggest dragon outside
a Chinese screen of one stroke,
meaning a nostril in the smoke
of water falling.

As tender – as baked meat in a stew.
It elevates its nose to the horizons
much as Chac's three hundred nose-
trunks unscroll and protrude: stony
Long Nose swatting up the Sun: three
hundred hard memos to the water demon.

Note: Puuc is the Mayan language of the area.